HOW TO DO MARKETING RESEARCH

PAUL N HAGUE
and
PETER JACKSON

**KOGAN
PAGE**

First published in Great Britain in 1990 by
Kogan Page Limited, 120 Pentonville Road,
London N1 9JN.

British Library Cataloguing in Publication Data
A CIP record for this book is available from the
British Library.

   ISBN 0-7494-0085-4
   ISBN 0-7494-0008-0 Pbk

Typeset by DP Photosetting, Aylesbury, Bucks
Printed and bound in Great Britain by
Martin's, Berwick upon Tweed

◀ CONTENTS ▶

◀ PREFACE ▶

Market research is a craft. Of course, the practitioner must understand the theory of the subject, but it is by actually *doing* that the market researcher gets better. And like all crafts, it takes time to become adept. It is, perhaps, no coincidence that job advertisements for market researchers frequently specify a minimum of two years' experience. Employers believe that this is a reasonable period to have 'served time'.

The aim of this book is to shorten the time it takes for the market researcher to become skilled. It is long on hints and wrinkles, and short on theory. It is a *workbook*, not a bible – the sort of book one would expect to see on a market researcher's desk as daily use is made of the checklists and specimen forms that are contained within it.

As we sat down to write this book, our minds were targeted on the people new to market research. However, in the process of writing, we found it very beneficial going over the old ground, reminding ourselves of the basic principles which sometimes get forgotten and are sometimes taken for granted. We hope, therefore, that skilled practitioners in market research will also find our book beneficial.

The core of our philosophy is that good market research is about asking the right questions of the right people. Not much more, not much less. We hope that this straightforward approach to market research is helpful to the new and experienced practitioner alike.

Paul Hague
Peter Jackson
Summer 1990

CHAPTER 1

PLANNING A MARKET RESEARCH PROJECT

In this chapter, we show how to plan a market research project. We start by considering the need for market research in the context of business decision-making. Next, we show how to plan a research exercise. Finally, we consider the resources needed to carry out a project.

This chapter applies equally to both consumer and business-to-business market research, and only a few differences between the two types of research are highlighted.

Market research and decision-making

Market research is the process of collecting, analysing and interpreting marketing information. Before discussing how to carry out market research, we should think about why marketing information is needed in a business.

Market research is the process of collecting, analysing and interpreting marketing information.

Running a business means taking decisions – all the time. Some of these decisions are trivial, with short-term consequences, and nothing very dreadful will happen if we get them wrong. Others, however, affect the long-term prospects or survival of the business. Whatever the scale or nature of the decision, a common thread is the need for information.

Imagine you are walking in the mountains. You reach a fork and have to decide whether to go left or right. Your decision will be made on the basis of the best information available to you at the time: what you have passed on your way to the fork, which of the alternatives looks the most trodden, what you can see ahead, and so on. You might, of course, make a poor decision and end at a precipice. In retrospect, you would realise that your misfortunate occurred because you lacked sufficient information. A map might have provided this.

Market research is one of the business 'maps' that guide the decision-maker. So it is in business. Information is needed to increase your chances of making the best decisions and market research is one of the business 'maps' that guide the decision-maker. Of course, this does not *guarantee* that you will always arrive at your targeted destination. The 'map' may lack the detail you need or it could be out of date.

Obviously, market research is concerned with decisions in the marketing function rather than in production, personnel or financial management. Because marketing is so central to any business, the consequences of marketing decisions inevitably spill over and affect other functions. Furthermore, the techniques used in market research can be applied in other areas such as personnel management – a topic outside the scope of this book.

1. What sorts of decision are marketing managers concerned with?

Some common decision areas where market research can help are as follows:

Opportunities
- What product should we offer?
- How should we formulate the product?
- How much should we charge?
- Which group of consumers are we going to supply?
- How will we get the product to our customers?
- How will we persuade consumers to buy our product rather than a competitor's?

Evaluation
- Can we increase sales of our product?
- Can we charge more for our product?
- Can we supply a different group of consumers?
- Should we change the way we get the product to customers?
- Should we change the way the product is offered?

Problem-solving
- How can we increase the profit made from a product?
- How can we reverse a trend of falling sales?
- How can we increase our customers' satisfaction with our products and service?

Each decision area involves making choices between alternatives and information is needed to assess the consequences. Many decisions are made on the basis of guesses or hunches, using information of a sort. The chances of making the best choice – the one that maximises future profits – are improved by having reliable information to hand.

Let us think about just one decision area: *How can I increase the profit made from a product?* This is a very common problem and in principle there are three strategies to pursue, either singly or in combination:

- Sell more of the product
- Charge more
- Reduce the cost of providing the product

There is a fourth option, however, and that is to change the method of accounting to show a better profit, but this has no market research implications.

In deciding whether or how to pursue any of these options, information is needed. This information may already be available from past research; alternatively, it may be necessary to carry out an exercise to collect it. Returning to our example decision area, the information needed to take a decision on increasing a product's profitability may be as follows:

Sell More
- Size of the total market in which we sell
- Our existing share of the market
- Availability of our product (retail distribution levels)
- Consumer awareness of our product
- Attitudes to our product

Charge more
- Competitors' pricing compared with ours

- Consumers' perception and 'valuation' of our product compared with competitors
- Effect of price increases on propensity to buy and so sales volumes
- Effect of price increases on availability/retail distribution

Cut costs
- Whether product reformulation is perceived by consumers
- And what effect does any such perception have on their valuation of the product?

All businesses face marketing problems. Write down *one* such problem in your own organisation (or imagine one) using the worksheet in Figure 1.1. Then, in the spaces given, list all the information you can think of (some of which you may already have) that seems relevant to making a decision to solve this problem. For now, think of the problem fairly generally and not just in the context of your own organisation. With only a bit of thought, you should be able to fill all the lines allotted for writing in the information.

Next, against each item of information, indicate whether your present

Statement of the problem

_____

_____

_____

Information needed   **Present level of knowledge**
                                      High   Medium   Low

_____   □   □   □

_____   □   □   □

_____   □   □   □

_____   □   □   □

_____   □   □   □

_____   □   □   □

Figure 1.1 *Worksheet: a marketing problem*

level of knowledge is: *high* – you are confident that the information you have available is complete and accurate enough; *medium* – you know something but it is incomplete or of doubtful accuracy; or, finally, *low* – you know nothing.

To help you think of the information relevant to a marketing problem, the following list outlines areas commonly covered in market research studies:

The market

- Total market size
- Who the consumers are (profiles of consumers)
- Consumers' needs and requirements
- Market segmentation by area, consumer grouping, needs or requirements
- Trends – a growing or declining market?

Types of information commonly provided through market research.

The market's structure

- The major players – domestic manufacturers, importers
- Branding
- Shares held by major players/brands
- How the market is serviced – distribution networks
- Major distributors and retailers
- Trends – who is growing, declining and why?

The suppliers and brands

- How the suppliers operate in the market
- Why they are successful (or not)
- Consumers' attitudes to (image of) suppliers and brands

The product

- Types of products sold within the market
- How the products are differentiated
- Relationship of products to market segmentation
- Level of product innovation
- Product life cycles – how long they last
- How the product meets consumers' needs
- Consumers' satisfaction with products
- The need to develop/change the product

15

New product development
- Unsatisfied needs and wants that could be met by a new product
- Acceptance of new product at concept, prototype or finished formulation stage
- Packaging of the new product
- How it should be presented to its market

Pricing
- Current pricing structures
- Past trends
- Consumers' attitude and sensitivity to pricing
- Consumers' price expectations for a product
- Anticipated changes in purchasing following price changes

Distribution/retailing
- Stocking policies
- Order frequencies
- Distribution levels achieved
- Delivery expectations
- Attitudes to suppliers, their products and service
- Marketing and merchandising policies

Sales methods
- Consumers' attitudes to the methods used
- Evaluation of different methods
- Relating market potential to sales organisation
- Sales organisation and market structure

Advertising
- Evaluation of advertising campaigns
- Audiences reached by advertising media
- Testing new advertising before/after use
- Relationship between advertising and product/brand perceptions

Having looked through this list of areas covered by market research, you should now return to thinking about the information needs of your own company – are there any other needs where you think market research information could help to improve decision-making?

This section has shown you the wide range of information that you *could* require to address marketing problems. Do remember, however, that

The process of obtaining information is to help you to arrive at a decision.

the process of obtaining information is to help you to arrive at a decision – it is *not* an alternative to decision-taking.

2. The relevance test

Many businesses stagger along without adequate information, but there are dangers the other way as well. Information collecting is a means and not an end, and its value depends on its *relevance* to the decision.

Information gathered must be relevant to the decision.

Think back to the marketing problem you identified within your own company and reconsider the relevance of the information you thought you needed to your own business. Some areas of information, while theoretically relevant to the problem, may not be particularly appropriate in the context of your business. For example, we suggested earlier that estimating market size could be important in deciding whether more of a product can be sold. This is true where the supplier has a significant share of the market. If you have a 50 per cent market share, it is important to know whether the market size is £80 million or £90 million per year. However, if you are a very small player, then the size of the total market (beyond a very broad estimate) is of little importance.

The relevance test should be applied to all information you are thinking of collecting. In market research, this test is applied by asking yourself how, having acquired certain information, it will help you to make a decision. If, by this test, the information is not useful, then probably it is not worth the time and trouble involved in collecting it.

Apply the relevance test to all information you are thinking of collecting.

By applying the relevance test, you should be able to cross out some of the information areas you thought might be useful to your company. It may help you to assign some priorities to those that remain, enabling you to rank them in order of importance. Without the application of this relevance test, there is a danger that information will be collected at both a time and a cost that will not help to make the decision.

It is not only businesses that have a need for marketing information. A charity, for example, raises funds through marketing activities and may need greater knowledge of why (or why not) people respond to its appeals. An association catering for members sharing a common leisure activity may face a falling roll and need to understand why this is so and how the trend can be reversed. Political groups also have 'products' and may need to understand how potential supporters perceive what is on offer.

17

Carrying out market research: a research plan

Anyone carrying out a market research project must have a plan.

Anyone carrying out a market research project must have a plan – a statement of what, why, when and how the work is to be done. If the project is to be carried out by an outside organisation, the plan is prepared and presented by that organisation, before the work is commissioned, in a *proposal* form. The proposal is a response to a *brief* given by the client. Such a brief is not necessarily a formal document although it is better if it is (see Chapter 8 for a fuller discussion of this topic).

An in-house market researcher also needs a research plan. Although there may be no need to 'sell' the project in the same way as an outside supplier of market research, it is good practice for the in-house researcher to prepare a formal, written and explicit plan which can be referred to by both the person carrying out the work and colleagues within the organisation. Everyone concerned will then understand the what, why, when and how of the work.

The elements of a research plan are as follows:

- Analysis of the requirement for research
- Statement of research objectives
- Information needed to meet the objective
- Research methods
- Project management
- Reporting
- Timetable
- Costs

The document setting out the research plan does not, of course, have to be organised so that it has separate sections corresponding in sequence to each of the elements. Authors have their own styles. However, all the subjects should be covered, in one form or another, in a thorough plan.

We now can consider each element of the research plan in turn.

1. Analysing the requirement for research

An analysis of the requirement for research should:

- Give some context – the business's involvement in the subject of the research.

- Briefly (and only briefly) describe any past events that led up to the present situation.
- State what the present situation is and how this fits in with wider business goals.
- Outline the decision options that are available.
- Indicate what information, relevant to the requirement, is available and what confidence can be put on it.

Figure 1.2 is an example of such an analysis. The product is deliberately

---

Our company manufactures the type of domestic appliance illustrated in the attached brochure. The products are marketed through wholesalers and Area Electricity Boards. There are considerable fixed resources devoted to the products' manufacture which cannot be easily switched to making different products.

Volume sales figures for our appliances are appended. Although there were fluctuations year to year, it will be seen that the long-term trend to 1982 was one of growth. Since 1983, sales have fallen every year and are now one-half the volume of 1982.

The marketing of this range now produces losses. Cost savings have been made, but sales revenue is now no longer sufficient to sustain the fixed costs entailed.

Options being considered include:

- Withdrawing from the market and closing the production unit
- Investment to create an efficient production unit at lower output levels
- Devoting resources to increasing sales volume
- Increasing prices to offset lower volumes

Statistics on all UK manufacturers' sales are available and are considered reasonably reliable. They indicate some decline since 1983 but not to the same degree as our own (summary appended). Comprehensive files are available providing product data on most similar equipment sold in the UK. A survey of retail pricing in major outlets (available) was carried out and this indicates that our own range is towards the cheaper end of the market but many imported products undercut us.

Figure 1.2 *Specimen analysis of a requirement for research*

left vague to encourage you to think about the general principles rather than particular issues.

The first paragraph tells us that the company manufactures a product, faces some restrictions in its response to changing market conditions (because of inflexible production) and tells us broadly how the product is sold. This short history introduces the current problem: sales are too

Context

_____

_____

_____

History

_____

_____

_____

Present situation

_____

_____

_____

Options

_____

_____

_____

Relevant information available

_____

_____

_____

Figure 1.3   _Worksheet: analysis of a requirement for research_

low to sustain fixed production costs. The future options are outlined. The data available indicates that the company is doing worse than other manufacturers, which suggests that its own actions are at least partly responsible. However, note that data is available on UK manufacturers' sales and there is no mention of imports or the total domestic market. Useful price data is also available.

The specimen analysis in Figure 1.2 is sufficient to enable us to set research objectives to help the company's management to choose the optimum decision from the options available.

Before moving on to the second element in the research plan (a statement of objectives), you should prepare your own analysis of a requirement for research. You can use the worksheet in Figure 1.3 which suggests some subheadings, but in any case try to keep to just one sheet.

2. Stating the research objectives

A statement of research objectives should describe what will be achieved by carrying out the research. These objectives should meet the business requirements covered in the preceding analysis stage and, in particular, they should provide information relevant to the options considered to be available. They should be precise but not too narrow.

> A statement of research objectives should describe what will be achieved by carrying out the research.

Returning to the example of the domestic appliance manufacturer, we can suggest four possible objectives for the research:

A   Provide an analysis of the market for domestic appliances of this type.
B   Establish consumers' attitudes to the company's and competitors' products.
C   Establish the effect of import penetration in the market for the domestic appliances.
D   Provide data that shows why sales of the product have fallen and which will enable the company to evaluate:
  ● means of increasing sales volume in future
  ● the potential to increase prices.

Like Father Bear's porridge bowl, A is just too large; it proposes to provide everything that can be found out about the market and by no means will everything be useful to the company. Furthermore, there is no attempt to relate what will be done in the research to the particular needs of the company. Arguably, also, there is a fault in the other direction. The extent of the data is not indicated and, therefore, almost anything provided could be said to meet the objectives. At the end of the exercise, it should be possible to evaluate whether or not the objective has been met.

The problem with both B and C is that they are too narrow. It may well be that the problem lies either in consumers' attitudes to the product on offer or that foreigners have stolen the business. Probably both issues need examining, but other factors may have led to the problems and must at least be thought about.

As in the story of the three bears, the last offering is judged just right. The problem facing the company is addressed, as are all the suggested options. You will recall that two of the objectives were essentially negative choices and presumably would be taken only if it was determined that the present trend could not be reversed.

3. Information needed to meet the objective

It is important to distinguish between the information needed to meet the objective and the objective itself.

It is important to distinguish between the information needed to meet the objective and the objective itself. The objective is a statement of an intention to provide data relevant to a marketing problem but, in itself, it does not indicate *what* the research must find out.

The research project is likely to be constrained by both time and costs, and it is quite possible that some compromises will have to be made in the depth and breadth of information that is sought. Furthermore, some information does not have to be sought, because it is already available. Figure 1.4 provides an example of a statement of information needs to meet the research objective set in the case of the domestic appliance company. All the information listed is relevant to explaining either why the company's sales have fallen or evaluating some possible option. This is made clear in italicised commentary.

The information in the specimen statement of objectives and information coverage is not comprehensive. With a little thought, it could be at least twice as long, but some judgement of what is important has been made. Even so, the range of information we propose to cover could prove too wide for our resources and the focus will have to be on just one or two areas, on the basis that these seem to be the *most relevant* to guiding a successful business decision.

Objectives

To provide data that shows why sales of the product have fallen and which will enable the company to evaluate the possibility of increasing sales volume or increasing prices.

Information coverage

(1) Analyse trends in UK manufacturers' sales and show the split between home and export sales.

Possibly the company has missed out on export sales.

(2) Analyse trends in the domestic market, including import penetration.

Sales may have fallen in line with the domestic market, possibly because of imports.

(3) Consider whether any new types of product have impacted on the market.

Perhaps the market has been lost to an innovatory new product.

(4) Show the structure of the retail market for appliances, including how it is supplied and any changes in the retail structure or policies.

The company may be missing new retail opportunities or not dealing well with them.

(5) Examine consumers' attitudes to the products and any requirements for product development.

Information in this area may help in product redesign.

(6) Show consumers' awareness of and attitudes to the company's and competitors' products.

Maybe the brand is just not known or regarded negatively.

(7) Analyse pricing and discount policies of suppliers.

While the retail price may be fairly low, there may be a problem in the deal offered to retailers.

(8) Establish consumers' attitudes to pricing and, specifically, to a significant increase in the company's own prices.

Will consumers pay higher prices?

Figure 1.4 *Specimen statement of objectives and information coverage for domestic appliance survey*

23

Planning the information coverage of the project is an exercise in hypothesis building. Each area to be covered implies a hypothesis about the cause of the problem facing a business. Thinking up hypotheses is an exercise in creativity; it is also one that is rooted in our knowledge and understanding of the situation. In theory, there is almost an infinite number of hypotheses to explain a given problem. However, based on our experience and understanding of the circumstances, we can usually make a reasonable attempt at selecting the few that are likely to be of most importance and perhaps arrange these in some order of priority. The limited research budget and timetable can then be allocated to best effect.

At this point, you may wish to prepare your own specimen statement of objectives and information coverage for your organisation (either real or imaginary).

4. Research methods

The research methods element of the plan describes *how* the work will be carried out. The tools required to collect the information in a study are the subject of the following chapters. An understanding of what can be obtained through desk research, how to plan fieldwork, the role of questionnaires and how to use them in interviewing is all needed before the research methods part of a plan can be written. There are, however, some general points that can be made about the different types of information sought and the effect this has on the choice of methods. The sources of research information are conveniently classified as either *primary* or *secondary*. It is convenient to think about them in reverse order.

Primary and secondary sources of information.

Secondary information is information that has already been collected, usually for some purpose quite unconnected with your own requirement. Generally, the information is in some published or semi-published form and is available through desk research (see Chapter 2). Information of this sort is often general and factual rather than particular and attitudinal. From published sources, we may obtain estimates of the size of a market for appliances and the extent to which imports have supplied this market. We are very unlikely to obtain any data on consumers' attitudes to the appliances and particular brands. The latter type of information requires special research among consumers of the appliances – in other words, primary research. Primary research may also be needed to collect general and factual information, or at least to refine data that is uncertain or too broad.

Quantitative data is an essential part of marketing decision-making. Without it, we have no concept of market size, brand shares, awareness and usage levels. A number of techniques are available for collecting quantitative data. In most cases, they involve a large number of interviews with a carefully chosen sample of individuals or organisations. The method of obtaining the data usually involves administering a structured questionnaire through face-to-face or telephone interviews, or perhaps a postal survey (although there are often problems here with the reliability of the sample). Later chapters describe each of these techniques.

Quantitative and qualitative data.

Qualitative data is also an important part of market research. In contrast to quantitative data, qualitative data is concerned with understanding the subjects of the research from within; it is very much concerned with attitudes and motivations. It concentrates on providing answers to the 'whys' and 'hows' rather than just the numbers. Examples of this sort of data include:

- How do consumers *feel* about using the appliance?
- What *attitudes* surround the purchase of the product?
- How is one brand rather than another *thought about*?

Qualitative data is concerned with attitudes but not all attitudinal data is qualitative. The question 'What do you think of this brand of appliance?' would be best approached in a qualitative way, but the related question 'Which brand is preferred overall?' needs a quantitative approach with a statistically reliable sample.

Sometimes, but not always, qualitative data is used to suggest hypotheses which are then tested by more rigorous quantitative methods. However, in practice, qualitative research is often used as a stand-alone method (and it has to be said that often the results have limited reliability because they are qualitative).

There are a number of qualitative techniques for the market researcher to choose from, but by far the most widely used is the group discussion (see Chapter 6).

In planning the research methods, you need to identify the type of information required (primary or secondary, quantitative or qualitative) and to make judgements about its availability.

In summary, therefore, planning the research methods requires you to identify what type of information you need and to make judgements about its availability. The information could be either:

- Primary or secondary data
- Quantitative or qualitative data

We are now in a position to restate the information coverage suggested for the domestic appliance company. This is presented in Figure 1.5. The implications of the choice of appropriate methods are made clear in italicised commentary. It should be noted that there is often uncertainty in the choice of methods; often there is no one ideal approach. The research activities suggested are quite extensive and the information coverage may need rethinking, especially in relation to the costs entailed.

In the methods section of the research plan, an outline description of the research tasks that will be carried out should be given, including a statement of the interviewing techniques and sample sizes. Figure 1.6 gives a specimen description based on research for the domestic appliance manufacturer. The plan is in outline rather than detail, but at the overall planning stage this will probably suffice. The research techniques mentioned are all discussed in later sections.

At this point, you may like to prepare a plan of research methods to meet your own statement of objectives and information coverage.

5. Project management and reporting

Project management and reporting needs only a brief mention in a research plan. The project management statement should indicate who will have overall responsibility for the project, who else will be involved and what other resources, if any, will be required.

At the research planning stage, it is desirable to think about how the research findings will be communicated to those involved in making the marketing decisions. The alternatives are a written report, in greater or lesser detail, or a verbal presentation of the results. Both approaches are often used together.

Figure 1.7 provides an example of this part of a research plan.

6. Timetable

A timetable is a necessary part of any research plan. The timetable should be realistic – one that *you* believe you can stick to. Constraints on a practical timetable include:

The project management statement should indicate who will have overall responsibility for the project, who else will be involved and what other resources, if any, will be required.

Think about how the research findings will be communicated to those involved in making the marketing decisions. The choices include a written report and/ or a verbal presentation.

The timetable should be realistic.

Project management
The manager of the market research department will be responsible for the project.

One full-time member of the department's staff will plan the work in detail, carry out desk research, lead the group discussions and organise the interview programmes.

A team of around 10–20 part-time interviewers will be required to carry out the interview programmes; this work will be subcontracted to a company able to provide this type of service. This organisation will also analyse completed questionnaires and produce tabulations of results.

Reporting
A brief summary report will be prepared. Tabulations from the analysis of interview questionnaires and group discussion transcripts will also be made available.

Results will be discussed in detail with company staff involved with the product.

Figure 1.7   *Specimen statement of project management and reporting*

- The time required to complete research tasks, given the resources available.
- The deadlines for taking the decisions which the research is guiding.

The deadlines may be set by external circumstances (for example, if the research is related to exercising a purchase option for a business) or just by a management whim. Indeed, there may be a conflict between the time necessary to carry out work of a suitable quality and a screamingly urgent deadline. Sometimes, with the best will in the world, the research may be impossible to carry out to an adequate standard within the time set by the management requiring the information. It is nearly always better to carry out no research if the alternative is to be a skimped and inadequate job.

Figure 1.8 shows a specimen timetable for the research into the domestic appliance market. The resources to be used are also indicated. Depending on the resources, some of the separate activities could be carried out consecutively or concurrently.

(1) Analyse trends in UK manufacturers' sales and show the split between home and export sales.

It is known that statistics on manufacturers' sales are available and possibly these are split by home and export. Desk research should, therefore, be an appropriate method.

(2) Analyse trends in the domestic market, including import penetration.

Import data is likely to be available from Customs & Excise. Again, therefore, desk research may be appropriate.

(3) Consider whether any new types of product have impacted on the market.

Some information is likely to be available in the trade press (desk research) plus perhaps 'overview' interviews (see Chapter 3 for an explanation of this term) with respondents close to this market.

(4) Show the structure of the retail market for appliances, including how it is supplied and any changes in the retail structure or policies.

Interviews with retailers including Area Electricity Boards will produce the data. Possibly a mix of telephone and face-to-face interviews will be appropriate.

(5) Examine consumers' attitudes to the products and any requirements for product development.

Qualitative research among consumers; probably a number of group discussions will be needed.

(6) Show consumers' awareness of and attitudes to the company's and competitors' products.

Interviews among a representative sample of consumers – possibly 'street' rather than in-home – will be adequate.

(7) Analyse pricing and discount policies of suppliers.

Retailer/distributor interviews are required; probably a common exercise to cover (4) as well.

(8) Establish consumers' attitudes to pricing and, specifically, to any increases in the company's own prices.

Qualitative research (group discussions) and/or interviews with a representative sample of consumers will be needed.

Figure 1.5 *Information coverage and choice of methods for domestic appliance survey*

General

The research will involve: desk research, interviews with retailers and distributors, group discussions with consumers and also a programme of street interviews.

Desk research

Desk research will be carried out to provide data on:

- Manufacturers' sales of the appliances
- Trends in the domestic market
- New products and their impact on the appliance

Desk research sources are likely to include trade association statistics, data from Customs & Excise and the trade press. Some 'overview' interviews will also be carried out.

Retailer and distributor research

Information to be covered through this type of research will be:

- The structure of the retail market
- The retail price structure

A total of 100 retailer and distributor interviews will be carried out: 10 face-to-face interviews (the larger retailers including some Area Electricity Boards) and 90 by telephone.

Qualitative research among consumers

Four group discussions will be held, each involving 8–10 respondents. The areas of information covered will be:

- Attitudes to products
- Consumers' attitudes to pricing

Consumer interviews

Consumer 'street' interviews will provide data on:

- Awareness and attitudes to products and brands
- Consumers' attitudes to pricing

A representative sample of 500 consumers will be interviewed.

Figure 1.6 *Specimen research methods for domestic appliance survey*

Activity	Resources	Days required
General planning and research design	1 member of staff	2–3
Desk research	1 member of staff	2–3
Retailer research (100 interviews)		
• Planning	1 member of staff	1
• Carrying out	10 interviewers	3–5
• Questionnaire analysis	1–2 members of staff	2
Group discussions (4)		
• Recruitment	4 interviewers (1 per group)	2–3
• Carrying out	1 member of staff	3–5
• Transcription of tapes	1 typist	2
Consumer interviews (500 street interviews)		
• Planning	1 member of staff	1
• Carrying out	10–20 interviewers	3–5
• Data analysis	2–3 members of staff	2–3
Report preparation (written summary and verbal presentation)	1–2 members of staff	3–5

Figure 1.8 *Specimen research timetable*

Always estimate the cost of research.

7. The budget/research costing

A costing should be part of the research plan, even when the majority of the work is to be carried out by in-house staff who are paid as an overhead (although it may be acceptable to quantify this in time rather than in money). Working out accurate costs depends on a realistic estimate of the resources needed and their cost. Figure 1.9 provides a useful worksheet for estimating costings. It is assumed that some services such as interviewers will be bought in, while other work will be carried out by overhead staff costed at notional internal rates. No allowance is made for adding a margin to the costs – this would obviously be done if the work is to be charged out to produce a profit.

Once the cost for a project has been estimated, it has to be checked against the available budget for the work. This will in turn reflect the

Activity	Man-days	Rate £	Cost £
Staff costs			
Internal staff			
• General planning and design	____	____	____
• Desk research	____	____	____
• Group discussions	____	____	____
• Fieldwork planning	____	____	____
• Questionnaire analysis	____	____	____
• Report preparation and presentation	____	____	____
Subtotal	____	____	____
Bought-in staff			
• Interviewing	____	____	____
• Other	____	____	____
Subtotal	____	____	____
Costs other than staff			
Staff expenses			____
• Travel			____
• Other			____
Printing			____
Interviewing services			____
Other services			____
Hire of venues and equipment			____
Directories and sampling frames			____
Subtotal			____
Other			____
Total	____		____

Figure 1.9 *Worksheet: specimen project costing sheet*

availability of funds, but it should also take account of the potential value of the research.

The costs have to be considered in the context of the profit or loss associated with the marketing decisions carried out as a result of the research. If, for example, the research is guiding a decision with an investment of say £50,000, then a research budget of several thousand pounds or more would be too much. If, however, an investment of

Costs have to be considered in the context of the profit or loss associated with the marketing decisions carried out as a result of the research.

31

£500,000 was involved, a larger research budget could be justified. In practice, estimating the likely pay-off from the research is not easy. This is particularly true when researching potential opportunities. Until the research is carried out, knowledge of the business potential is slight.

On occasions, the estimated costs of the 'ideal' research plan are more than the available budget or the estimated pay-off from the project. In such cases, either the research methods must be trimmed or the range of information being sought must be scaled down. This may well be appropriate in our domestic appliance example. It is important to bear in mind that squeezing the timetable and budget could result in the quality of the research output being so compromised that it is better not to carry out the work at all.

Resources required

Expertise is essential. This book provides it for you.

The key resource needed to carry out any market research project is expertise. This book is designed to give you some of this essential commodity. Beyond that, what is needed is the necessary staff time to carry out a particular project. Market research, in most respects, is still a very labour-intensive activity and, outside data analysis (especially processing of questionnaires), the information technology revolution has had limited impact.

Market research can be carried out by specialist market research organisations (perhaps for some aspects, if not the whole of a project). The use of agencies is discussed further in Chapter 8. If the project is carried out in-house, the human resources required depend very much on what is to be done and the time available.

The following sections give some guidance on how long different types of research activities require. Taking this into account, and the timetable available, the number of staff needed can be estimated and, if necessary, recruited on a short-term basis. With the right contacts to find temporary additional staff, even a research department of one can organise quite large projects.

1. Desk research

Desk research is subject to diminishing returns. In a typical project, say the domestic appliance example, two man-days spent in a library, supplemented by perhaps one or two carrying out telephone 'overview' interviews, would produce most of the data.

2. Telephone interviews

The number of telephone interviews that can be carried out in a day is often more dependent on the time needed to locate appropriate respondents than on the length of the interview itself. In business-to-business research, it may be necessary to make several calls to a company to locate a suitable respondent (and find him or her in). In consumer research, the respondent may have to qualify for an interview in some way – for example, be an owner occupier or have bought a certain brand of a product – before fitting the quota of respondents being interviewed. Some idea of the likely level of 'qualified' respondents in the total population is needed in order to estimate the number of unfruitful calls that will be encountered in a survey (for example, in a survey of owner occupiers about 60 per cent would qualify).

It is important, therefore, to give some thought to the likely 'strike' rate for each job. For both business-to-business and consumer telephone interviews, it is reasonable to assume that finding the right respondent will take at least as long as carrying out the interview. On this basis, we can expect to carry out, say, two telephone interviews per hour if the actual interview duration is 15 minutes or 10 to 12 in a six-hour day (not many people will work at telephone interviewing for more than six hours per day). Therefore, with one person available for the work, a programme of 100 interviews could require 10 days. Taking into account interviewer fatigue, however, research programmes of this scale are unlikely to be completed by a one-person team.

The time needed for interviewing.

3. Face-to-face interviews

In face-to-face interviews, considerable time can be spent in travelling. In business-to-business research, with a programme of interviews among a small but nationally spread sample (for example, manufacturers of batteries), only one or two interviews might be achieved per day. This could be increased to four or five per day if the respondent sample is geographically clustered in city centres (for example, solicitors' practices). In any case, face-to-face interviews of this sort are expensive in time and, therefore, costs.

Consumer interviews, carried out in the home, among a pre-selected sample, face similar problems. If pre-selected addresses are not used, the achievement rate increases. Very often, interviewers are told to interview a certain number of respondents matching specific demographic criteria. This is known as a *quota sample*. Finding people to fit the various quotas becomes progressively harder as the interviewer nears completion of the job.

The time needed for interviews.

Quota problems apart, street interviews tend to be the most cost-effective method of consumer quantitative research with perhaps the time spent finding respondents reduced on average to around one-half the interview duration time. On a good day with an easy quota (or none), an interviewer can achieve around 40 street interviews with an average duration of five minutes. (This assumes a six-hour working day.) A programme of 500 such interviews would require 10 to 12 interviewer days. It is likely that a number of areas would be covered in the interviewing – research in, say, five major towns would require two or three days' work for one interviewer per town.

4. Group discussions
Group discussions are within the capability of a small research team (while research among large samples is not). It is possible to plan two group sessions per evening (each lasting one to one-and-a-half hours) and, therefore, eight groups can be covered in a week. Each group must be *recruited*; for a consumer group this can take one interviewer one or two days, while a business-to-business research group will take considerably longer. Group proceedings are taped and staff time is needed for transcription.

5. Postal surveys
These also can be carried out by a small team – even one person – although temporary staff might be drafted in to help with the mailing.

6. Data analysis
Even if computers are available, any type of research involving the use of standard questionnaires requires resources for coding and the analysis of completed questionnaires (see Chapter 7). As an indication of the scale of staff time required, 500 four-page questionnaires with two or three open-ended questions might require at least seven man-days' work to prepare and enter the data into a computer.

With experience, estimates of the time and, therefore, the staff resources needed to complete a project within a timetable can be made. A

Activity	Resources	Output rate	Days required
Desk research	_____	Not applicable	_____
Group discussions			
● Planning/recruitment	_____	_____	_____
● Carrying out	_____	_____	_____
Fieldwork	_____	_____	_____
Data analysis	_____	_____	_____
Other	_____	_____	_____

Figure 1.10 *Worksheet: specimen resource planning sheet*

resource planning sheet such as that shown in Figure 1.10 can be used.

Resource planning is clearly linked to both budgeting and setting a timetable, and the resource sheet suggested can be linked to the project costing sheet shown in Figure 1.9.

Resource planning is clearly linked to both budgeting and setting a timetable.

The equipment resources that are required to carry out market research tend to be few and non-specialised; all can be bought in as services. Where data in any volume has to be processed, a specialised software package (see Chapter 7) that runs on a personal computer could be considered.

◀ CHAPTER 2 ▶

DESK RESEARCH

There is no point reinventing the wheel. In market research terms, desk research is a wheel that someone else has invented and which could prove useful to the researcher if it can be unearthed. In this chapter, we show the uses of desk research, show where to look for information and give checklists that could help the researcher in the search.

The term *desk research* is self-descriptive. It is research, especially using information that has already been published, that in the main is carried out from a desk. It is sometimes referred to as secondary data to distinguish it from primary data (see Chapter 1), which is raw data obtained by fieldwork (see Chapter 3). However, within the definition of desk research, we would include discussions with trade associations and similar 'overview' interviews.

Desk research can be carried out quickly and at low cost.

Desk research is particularly useful to market researchers because it can be carried out quickly and at a low cost. Unfortunately, it is not always possible to know in advance whether or not the information can be found. You must be prepared for your efforts to be fruitless from time to time. However, it is a rare study that is totally barren, and more often than not the yield is heavy.

The uses of desk research

Some surveys can be carried out almost entirely by desk research. Let us imagine that your boss asks you to find out what you can about the market for plastic packaging for food before tomorrow night. In these circumstances, you are almost bound to rely on desk research, as there is too little time to organise a survey. A report prepared from desk research will vary in quality according to the availability of information, how up to date it is and the time that is available to piece it together.

A good desk researcher not only knows the sources of information, but is also imaginative in the way that the data is used. For example, a company may be interested in the use of plastics in food packaging. There may be little or no published data specifically on the market for plastics in food packaging but there may be plenty on the markets that use the products – that is, yoghurts, yellow fats, soft drinks, etc. Simply acquiring a few products, weighing the empty yoghurt pots, the margarine tubs, butter containers and the drinks bottles, and multiplying by the number of items sold (which is readily available data) will give a crude indication of the market for plastic raw materials in food sectors. In this way, you can obtain information on the market for products for which there is no information *through association* with other products where there is data available.

A good desk researcher not only knows the sources of information, but is also imaginative in the way that the data is used.

Desk research is often used alongside primary methods of data collection in the preparation of market research reports.

The following list outlines five important areas where desk research can make a major contribution:

- In selecting a sample. Published sources list people or companies to interview and can be found in the electoral register, the telephone directory, lists of past customers and trade directories.
- Obtaining details on products. Desk sources of information on products are: observation (looking at what is in use or in the shops); buying products and stripping them down (weighing the yoghurt pots!); obtaining sales literature on products; looking at adverts for products, etc.
- Providing an economic backcloth to a study. Market research reports may need some background as a perspective against which the primary information can be set. A survey on the use of plastics in food containers may be made more understandable by a section that describes trends in food packaging in general. The broader the scope, the more likely there is to be something available in published form.
- In the assessment of market size and trends. The government, trade

Five important uses for desk research.

associations and market research companies publish reams of statistics on the production, import, export and sales of products. Sometimes these statistics are only the starting point for the analysis of the market, especially if the product of interest occupies a small and narrow niche. It may well be necessary to find out an accurate market size figure by carrying out a field survey.

● Providing information on companies. Desk research can yield a considerable amount of information on companies. It can show their turnover and financial performance, the structure of their management, the products they sell, how they advertise, their distribution networks, their prices, etc. This information can be found in company accounts, press cuttings, product literature, directories and articles in journals.

Where to find the data

In one respect, carrying out desk research is made easy because much of the data is brought together in libraries or is available from commercial databases. A good library will contain, under one roof, most directories. It will have 'clippings' files on industries, Extel cards on companies, and journals and magazines on all manner of subjects.

On-line databases (discussed in more detail at the end of this chapter) bring together a host of information from newspapers, journals and market research reports. They allow market researchers to rapidly scan vast files for a modest cost. A wide variety of databases can be selected on the basis of:

● Source (some cover just one or two journals)
● Product (some cover products such as rubber and plastics or chemicals)
● Disciplines (some cover marketing subjects, others cover engineering)
● Companies (some are on-line 'directories')

Besides libraries and on-line databases, there are many other sources of desk research. Financial information can be obtained from Companies House and statistical information from the Central Statistical Office. In addition, observation in the shops and the streets can be very rewarding.

We now describe the many sources of information with which the desk researcher should be familiar.

1. The government as a source of information

The government collects data on almost everything, from our social habits through to the things we produce. It needs this information to control and guide the economy. As a by-product, the information becomes available to the general public at either no cost or a fraction of the cost of collection. The Central Statistical Office is the pivot of the information-collection process, bringing together the information-gathering services of the Business Statistics Office and the Office of Population Censuses and Surveys.

Government offices collect data on almost everything.

Many government publications can be purchased for quite nominal sums from HM Stationery Office, which has shops in all major cities. There are two publications that are well worth buying from HMSO:

- *Guide to Official Statistics.* This is a source book showing what is available from different government publications.
- *Annual Abstract of Statistics.* This publication is the annual version of the *Monthly Digest of Statistics*, giving information on the economy, demography, construction and industrial output.

An important source of data on manufacturing industry is the *Business Monitor*, produced by the Business Statistics Office. This is a series of statistical reports on the output of British manufacturing industry and it is the place to which most industrial market researchers turn if they want to know the size of a market. The *Business Monitors* are organised according to the *Standard Industrial Classification* (very often referred to as SIC) which is a system devised by the government to group different types of businesses.

Consumer market researchers may find some market size data in government statistics but, by and large, they turn to private sources. Market research companies such as AGB, Neilsen and BMRB carry out audits and continuous surveys on most household items, food and drink. Mintel and Euromonitor publish monthly surveys on a wide range of consumer products and these can be purchased for a relatively small sum. Handbooks from the Advertising Association and the *Daily Mirror* are worth acquiring as they are small compendiums of frequently referred to consumer-marketing research data on subjects like the structure of the population, market sizes, media circulation figures, etc.

2. Customs & Excise as a source of information

The government has privatised some of its data analysis departments. Information on imports and exports is one such area. Such information is handled by six companies who will prepare analyses of data for a small fee. Information that can be obtained from these agents is:

- Annual or monthly trade statistics at tariff/trade, commodity code number or Standard International Trade Classification level
- The identity of importers by commodity code number

Import and export data helps to identify export targets or shows where low-cost competition originates.

Import and export data is useful to market researchers because it shows the sources of products coming into the country and the destinations of products leaving it. Since the value and volume of the imports and exports are also recorded, the average selling prices of the goods at the dockside can be calculated. This helps to identify export targets or shows where low-cost competition originates.

Here are some hints on how to make Customs & Excise data work for your company:

- Find out the Customs Nomenclature into which your company's type of products is classified by speaking to one of the companies that prepares the analysis (or look it up in the nomenclature book held in most public libraries).
- Obtain an analysis of the imports and exports of the products your company makes for the last complete year, from one of the data preparation companies. (If you order December's figures, you will get that month plus the year to date.)
- Look at where the exports are going and the imports are coming from. Work out the average export prices and see if they suggest any attractive markets.

3. Directories as a source of information

Directories can be used to obtain information on competitors, suppliers and customers.

Market researchers in both industrial and consumer companies use directories to obtain information on competitors, suppliers of equipment or raw materials and, of course, customers.

Trade directories are the most common source of information on other companies. The most important of these are:

- *Kompass*. This directory is now in three volumes with the first listing over 25,000 companies and the products they make. The second lists 30,000 companies grouped by town and county; it gives a profile of their management. The third contains a summary of financial information on the largest companies. *Kompass* is also available on-line, providing a rapid source of information on UK and European companies.

- Dun & Bradstreet. This publisher offers a number of directories, the most famous of which is *Key British Enterprises*. This contains a financial summary, trade names, the names of directors and the major product groupings for the top 20,000 companies in the UK. The directory is also available on-line and is useful for credit checks and obtaining financial accounts on companies (including those in most countries in the European Community).

- *Who Owns Whom.* This directory provides the genealogical trees of most large companies. It enables researchers to determine the parents and subsidiaries of firms in the UK.

In addition to these very popular directories, every researcher is likely to have a favourite, specific to an industry. *Freight Industry Yearbook*, *Retail Trades Directory*, the *Computer Users Yearbook* are all, respectively, at the right hand of researchers in the transport industry, the retail trade and the electronics industry.

4. The press as a source of information

The local, national, daily and weekend newspapers carry information that may be useful to the market researcher. Adverts within the press are a shop window of what is being offered and how companies are positioning themselves. Comment in the financial pages of the national press, especially the *Financial Times*, is a fertile source of information on public companies and the larger private firms. Some of the information may relate to half-yearly or annual results, while press releases (which get published) tell more general stories about companies.

The press can be a valuable source of information on companies.

The local press should not be forgotten as a source of information on companies. Companies that are too small to receive mentions in the national press enjoy a much fuller local coverage.

5. Trade journals as a source of information

Every industry has two or three trade journals. The journals are published weekly or monthly and are crammed with stories on companies, sometimes based on genuine editorial analysis, but more often they are straight copies of press releases. Back copies of the trade journals can be obtained from libraries or from the publishers themselves.

6. Companies House as a source of information

Financial information on companies can be obtained from Companies House. This can be used to assess the turnover of a company and its market size.

Companies House is based in the City of London and has its major archives at Cardiff. Every limited liability company and public company has to file a set of audited accounts within 10 months and 7 months, respectively, of their year ends. These accounts are kept together with other financial data on the companies such as the Memorandum of Association (it says what the company can and cannot do) and the Share Register (which tells you who owns the company).

Researchers analysing the structure of a market often make use of the profit and loss accounts filed at Companies House as a source of the turnover of companies. By estimating the proportion of turnover attributed to a particular group of products and adding together the figures for all the players in the market, an assessment can be made of the market size. Since the Companies Act of 1981, researchers' guns have been spiked as 'small companies' can escape all but a very terse disclosure statement, which gives little away. 'Small' within the context of the disclosure requirements of Companies House means those companies with a turnover not exceeding £2 million, those employing no more than 50 people or those having a net worth of no more than £0.975 million. Even companies that fit the description 'medium' (that is, up to £8 million turnover, 250 employees and net worth of £3.9 million) can avoid providing their turnover figure if they want – although most do provide it as a matter of course. Thus, only the largest companies are now obliged to disclose turnover figures and this can be a serious limitation to a market researcher studying a sector where the majority of companies are modest in size. However, it is usually worth examining the financial reports of all classes of company, as even the smallest have to provide a balance sheet (albeit abbreviated) and some clues to its activities may be deduced. Information can be culled by any member of the public from the microfiches that are held on every limited liability company at Companies House. The researcher may retain the microfiche copy or, alternatively, the microfiche on a company's file can be ordered by telephone and sent by post for a nominal sum.

Obtain the accounts of three of your main competitors and complete the

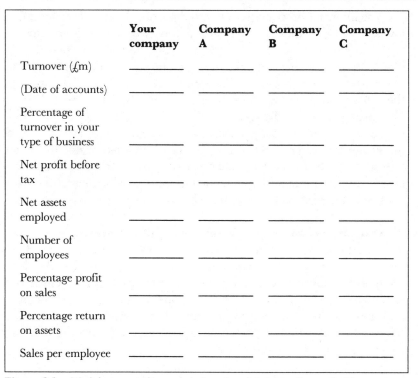

	Your company	Company A	Company B	Company C
Turnover (£m)	————	————	————	————
(Date of accounts)	————	————	————	————
Percentage of turnover in your type of business	————	————	————	————
Net profit before tax	————	————	————	————
Net assets employed	————	————	————	————
Number of employees	————	————	————	————
Percentage profit on sales	————	————	————	————
Percentage return on assets	————	————	————	————
Sales per employee	————	————	————	————

Figure 2.1 *Worksheet: competitor analysis from financial data at Companies House*

worksheet in Figure 2.1. It contains a number of ratios of financial performance which show the 'health' of your company against its rivals. They are based on four key measures of performance – turnover, net profit before tax, the capital employed to run the business (sometimes referred to as net assets) and the number of employees.

7. Trade associations as a source of information

There is a trade association for just about every business imaginable. Indeed, the *Directory of British Associations* published by CBD Research lists over 6300. Trade associations are self-help groups that originally looked after their members' interests, amassing production and sales figures in the days before the government took over this role. Thus, the older trade associations are usually larger and more powerful, and they have a deeper involvement in the collection of statistics than the new ones.

Where trade associations do not perform 'number crunching', they assume a role of lobbying the government with their causes or they

Find out which trade association is directly or indirectly connected with a business. Look them up and find out what they can offer.

43

provide information packs to interested parties. Their role is very often low key and the officials who head them may only work part-time.

Trade associations are not always the helpful source of information that market researchers hope for. They may not have the data themselves; they may not release data to non-members; they may have a membership that has changed over the years; the data they do have may be partial, if there are some operators who are not members. However, in certain traditional industries – vehicle manufacturing, the metal industries, textiles and construction materials – trade associations are large, powerful and useful sources of information. Elsewhere, they are at least worth getting to know to see what they can offer.

8. Your own company as a source of information

The sales performance of a company is due partly to its marketing efforts in a competitive environment and partly to the result of trends within the market. Plotting a company's sales over time may give a clue to the shape and movement of the market. If one product group is declining and another one is increasing, this could be an indication of what is happening in the market as a whole. It is at least a reason for researching the market to test this hypothesis.

Every company should make an effort to track its performance against the size of the market – and in so doing, plot its market. Changes in market share are signals for action.

Every company should make an effort to track its performance against the size of the market – and in so doing, plot its market share. Changes in market share are signals for action. An increase in market share may mean that a promotional campaign is working; that a competitor is on the decline; or it could mean that a product is priced too low. A decline in market share may mean that a product has been usurped by the competition; that competitors are more aggressive in their marketing; or it could be an indication of poor distribution and prices that are too high. In any event, plotting the company's sales against the market should raise questions and it may prompt an investigation.

Complete the worksheet in Figure 2.2 by entering your company's sales figures for a product group on which you also have market size data over a number of years. Calculate your company's market share for each year. Now consider why the market share has changed from year to year. If you are not sure, it could be worth carrying out research to find out why.

Market researchers are surrounded by a wealth of information on

Year	Market size	Company sales	Percentage of market share
1985	_____	_____	_____
1986	_____	_____	_____
1987	_____	_____	_____
1988	_____	_____	_____
1989	_____	_____	_____
1990	_____	_____	_____

Figure 2.2   *Worksheet: an exercise every company should carry out – plotting market share trends*

markets *within* their companies. Representatives' call reports contain information relating to the needs of particular customers but they may also have information about the performance of products, what people are buying, what competitors are doing and the changing requirements of the market.

Senior executives often visit competitors' factories and sit on standards committees. If they minute what they have learned, the information could be brought together by the in-house market researcher to tell a much larger story.

9. Market research reports as a source of information

Many market research companies take initiatives to produce reports that they subsequently publish for a few hundred or thousand pounds. This comparatively low cost for marketing information is made possible because many clients buy the reports. The British Overseas Trade Board (Department of Trade and Industry) publishes a listing of multi-client market research reports in a booklet entitled *Marketsearch/ The International Directory of Published Market Research*. This directory gives a brief description of the contents of each report, its price, the number of pages, and the names and addresses of the companies offering them for sale. Anyone interested in a report can contact the market research company that has published the document and ask for a table of contents and further details on the information coverage. Most market research companies will allow a prospective buyer to examine a report at their offices.

Consult The International Directory of Published Market Research for a listing of available market research reports.

Multi-client reports are always good value for money because they are inexpensive compared with *ad hoc* commissions. However, they sometimes fail to satisfy buyers because their expectations of the reports' coverage are unrealistic. Multi-client reports are often quite general as they are aimed at a wide market. The buyer of multi-client reports should take them for what they are – a good introduction to a subject which may raise questions that *ad hoc* research can answer.

Searching for published information on market size

Market researchers often have to rely on desk research to find information on market size. Market size data may be found in convenient form in reports sold by Mintel, Euromonitor, AGB, Neilsen or BMRB, or information published in *Business Monitors*, or it could be found in one-off government reports such as those carried out by the Monopolies & Mergers Commission. Articles in journals may refer to market sizes that the author has assessed or which are attributed to a published market research study, such as those listed in *The International Directory of Published Market Research.*

If the researcher cannot find any published estimates of market size, it may be necessary either to:

● Make estimates by grossing up data on users

or, more likely:

● Find out the turnover of companies that supply the products (by talking to the companies themselves, or by referring to their accounts at Companies House or to directories) and add them up
● Make estimates of the turnover of (manufacturing) companies by finding out how many people they employ (this data is published in directories such as *Kompass*) and multiplying this by what seems a reasonable sales per employee figure for the industry as a whole

Figure 2.3 outlines the steps involved in assessing market size from a company's estimated turnover.

Desk research requires a creative approach as the researcher must make as much as possible of the limited information available. Sometimes, interpretations have to be made from partial data, perhaps on a related

(1) List all the large- and medium-sized companies that operate in the market.

(2) For each company, find out, from Companies House (or from directories or make an estimate), the total (UK and export) turnover in all products. Note the year of the turnover figures and try to estimate what each company could be turning over *this year*.

(3) For each company, estimate the current UK turnover in the market/ product you are researching.

(4) Make an estimate of the combined current turnover in the UK for the market/product of interest for all the small companies that you have not listed.

(5) Add the estimates of UK turnover in the product group of interest to obtain the market size.

Company name	Total turnover	UK turnover
————————	————————	————————
————————	————————	————————
————————	————————	————————
————————	————————	————————
————————	————————	————————
Other (small companies)	————————	————————
Total	————————	————————

Figure 2.3 *Worksheet: how to assess market size from companies' turnover*

subject. It is difficult, therefore, to present a precise formula for carrying out desk research to determine market size. However, by following a number of steps, the researcher can apply logic to the search. The checklist in Table 2.1 suggests a course of action for determining a market size from desk research.

In a similar way, a step-by-step approach can be applied to the search for information on products or companies. Action checklists for studying these subjects are shown in Tables 2.2 and 2.3.

Table 2.1   *Checklist to determine market size by desk research*

Step	Action	If unsuccessful
1	Examine *Business Monitor*.	Phone *Business Monitor* at Cardiff; to step 2.
2	From *Guide to Official Statistics*, search for other government source of statistics.	To step 3.
3	Identify and contact relevant trade association from *Directory of Associations*.	Obtain leads from trade association; to step 4, 5, 6 or 7.
4	Search articles in trade magazines and press using McCarthy's or an abstracting service.	Phone relevant journal for leads; to step 5, 6 or 7.
5	Build up list of UK turnover of companies from Companies House, Dun & Bradstreet and Extel; make estimates of proportion of turnover derived from product of interest.	To step 6 or 7.
6	Determine if any correlation exists with other products or employment; seek data on that product or employment base as per step 2.	To step 7.
7	Check in directories of published market research for availability of multi-client report.	Consider fieldwork survey to discover market size.

Searching for information using on-line databases

Research time can be considerably reduced by using on-line databases.

Desk research is a quick way of building up information on a market – far quicker than using primary methods such as interviewing. Even so, conventional desk research, involving library searches, can take a number of days. This can be reduced to just a few minutes by using on-line databases.

On-line databases are commercially operated files of information that can be accessed, by anyone with a password, from a personal computer. Fees are charged on a 'pay-as-you-go' basis for either pieces of information or, more normally, for the time spent searching on-line. The *Financial Times*, for example, is held on a database called *Profile*. A

Table 2.2   *Checklist to obtain product information by desk research*

Step	Action	If unsuccessful
1	Write to company asking for brochures, data sheets and prices.	Contact distributors for same information.
2	Search trade journals and appropriate media for adverts, editorial mentions, articles and product reviews.	Contact journals as a check; try abstracting service; to step 3.
3	Search buyers' guides and directories for product specifications and background.	To step 4 or 5.
4	Buy or rent sample product for testing (obviously impractical for large or expensive items) or take photographs of products at dealers or end-users.	To step 5.
5	Search for exhibitions to visit where product may be displayed.	Consider commissioning study to find users of product.

researcher wanting to find any information reported on a company or a subject can, within minutes, look through hundreds of copies of the newspaper by entering a word (or a string of words) as a search command. This is a 'full text' database, which means that the whole of the articles in the newspaper are held and can be searched. Other databases contain synopses of articles so that a researcher can quickly consider the key subjects and order full texts of the articles if they seem interesting.

Database searches of broad subjects can produce hundreds of references. These can be reduced to a more manageable number by confining the search to articles published within a certain period (say, the last three months). Thereafter, records can be pruned by adding more specific terms to the search. For example, a survey of 'green' (as in environmental) issues would yield thousands of references, even over a short period. The researcher could make the references more appropriate by picking out only those containing the words 'packaging' and 'food' in the same article.

Table 2.3 *Checklist to obtain information on a company or companies*

Step	Action	If unsuccessful
1	Obtain accurate name, address and telephone number from a directory or buyers' guide; phone reception to check on accuracy.	Question Directory Enquiries, competitive company, distributor, known end-user in case of change of name or address; to step 2.
2	Assemble basic data on date of formation, product range, subsidiary companies, parent, number of employees, directors, financial status, etc, from *Kompass*, Dun & Bradstreet, *Who Owns Whom*; build up list of distributors from adverts in Yellow Pages or buyers' guides.	Check with distributors, competitors or other companies that may know; to step 3.
3	Check for Monopolies Commission reports on the industry and industry reports published in *Financial Times*; obtain copies.	To step 4.
4	Write to company's publicity department for corporate brochure and literature.	Try sales department or distributor; to step 5.
5	Obtain largest Ordnance Survey map of factory site; blow up to give plan of site, access and area for expansion.	Photograph site; to step 6.
6	For quoted company, write to company secretary for report and accounts.	Obtain accounts from Companies House.
	For unquoted company, obtain financial profile and microfiche from Companies House (make sure the precise name is applied for).	If 'non-trading', try to find trading company and obtain accounts; to step 7.
7	Search trade journals and all media for adverts, articles and references including local papers close to works or head office; record management appointments.	Try abstracting service; to step 8.
8	Check with trade association if technical symposia have included papers given by company; obtain papers.	Consider fieldwork to profile the company.

Some databases are *electronic directories* containing information on companies. These can be useful for pulling out samples for business-to-business surveys, as it is easy to select by industry, geographical area or company size (measured in terms of number of employees or turnover). Equally, such databases can be useful for obtaining background information on competitors and customers. Both *Kompass* and Dun & Bradstreet are available on-line and the researcher can select simple data, such as a name and address, through to detailed information on companies' management structure and financial performance.

Many city and business school libraries will carry out on-line database searches for the cost of the search itself plus a handling charge. Since the researchers are regularly carrying out database searches, and are therefore highly skilled, they are likely to be able to carry out a search far cheaper than most market researchers.

A number of database suppliers useful to market researchers are listed in the Appendix.

◀ CHAPTER 3 ▶

FIELDWORK PLANNING

Although the objectives of a market research study may in some cases be met through desk research alone, fieldwork is usually needed to collect the required data. This chapter tells you how to plan a programme of fieldwork.

Strictly speaking, not all types of fieldwork involve interviewing – for example, data can be collected by postal surveys. However, for convenience, we use the term 'interviewing' and 'fieldwork' interchangeably. Respondent selection and sampling are an important part of fieldwork, and they too are discussed in this chapter. We conclude by providing some guidance on how to plan and control a fieldwork programme.

Classification of fieldwork

A number of fieldwork methods are available to the market researcher and it can be helpful to describe briefly their different roles. The techniques are covered in more detail in Chapters 4, 5 and 6.

Fieldwork may be classified into three major divisions according to how the data collection is carried out:

Face to face

Consumer research

- Quantitative
  - Street interviews
  - In-home interviews
  - Placements
  - Hall tests
- Qualitative
  - Group discussions
  - Depth interviews

Business-to-business research

Place of work interviews
Clinics
Group discussions
Overview interviews

Telephone

- Stand-alone
- With visits or postal survey

Non-interviewing methods

- Postal survey
- Observation

Face-to-face interviewing involves a meeting between the person collecting the data (the interviewer) and the person giving it (the respondent). In consumer research, individual interviews may be carried out in the respondent's home or in the 'street'. The street may be a shopping precinct or another area where respondents are available to be interviewed.

Face-to-face interviewing.

Interviews with the general public may also be carried out in a *hall* – a place where respondents are brought for interview, usually because they are to be shown, handle or taste something. Alternatively, respondents could be asked to consider a product through a *home placement*. Some products cannot be tested in a hall; for example, if an opinion is sought after prolonged use of personal products.

The face-to-face interviews discussed so far are carried out on a one-to-one basis between the interviewer and the respondent. In group discussions, the interviewer's role changes to that of leader or 'moderator' of typically five to ten respondents. Group discussions are a 'depth' or 'qualitative' technique and an alternative to individual depth interviews.

Face-to-face interviews in business-to-business research are normally carried out in the respondent's place of work. When business-to-business respondents are brought to a venue, this approach is sometimes referred to as a *clinic*, as opposed to a hall test. The group discussion approach is equally useful in business-to-business research where qualitative data is sought. The task of leading a consumer or business-to-business group discussion is similar, but the recruitment techniques are rather different. In either case, recruitment is a major but hidden part of the work involved.

In-depth interviewing is also used in qualitative business-to-business research. As in consumer interviewing, individuals give their own personal view or perhaps the collective view of the organisations they represent. An important variant, however, is the *overview* interview, which is carried out with an 'expert' who provides information about a market as a whole or some aspect of it. For example, the marketing director of a leading supplier could be asked to give his estimate of market size and suppliers' shares.

Telephone interviews.

Telephone interviews can be carried out in both consumer and business-to-business research, either as a stand-alone method, or in conjunction with visits (as a preliminary or follow-up) or a postal survey.

Postal surveys.

A *postal survey* can also be used in both consumer and business-to-business research. Combining a postal survey with telephone interviews can overcome some of the limitations of each individual method: the telephone can be used to identify relevant respondents and increase co-operation; a self-completion questionnaire sent through the post, together with illustrations, can be used to communicate a product visually and obtain answers to scalar questions (see Chapter 7).

Other *non-interviewing fieldwork* methods include observation of people (for example, how a product is used) or things (for example, retail displays).

Selection of an appropriate fieldwork method

We now consider why and when to use one fieldwork method rather than another. A number of factors are relevant and in a study it may often be necessary to make a compromise to resolve conflicting requirements.

1. Information
The nature of the information is a most important factor to consider.

The difference between quantitative and qualitative data has already been discussed (see Chapter 1). Quantitative data usually requires the collection of standardised data from a reliable and representative sample. Either face-to-face or telephone interviews can be considered. In a business-to-business project, it may be desirable to use both methods, with visits to the most important respondents and telephone interviews to cover the rest. Avoid, however, mere 'token' visits carried out to impress somebody.

The type of information sought is an important factor to consider.

The nature of the data sought must also be considered. Some information just cannot be reliably collected over the telephone, as the respondent may need to check records or the interviewer may have to observe something.

Attitude measurement using scales is a type of quantitative data, often based on a large number of interviews. Face-to-face interviews, perhaps with a self-administered part to the questionnaire, are clearly an appropriate method for obtaining scalar responses. Telephone interviews are more restrictive – long 'batteries' of questions and scales of more than three points do not work well. Sometimes postal surveys can be considered as an alternative. However, in the main, face-to-face interviewing is required for obtaining attitude measurements.

Methods appropriate for collecting qualitative data include depth interviews and groups. Qualitative research and groups are often thought to be synonymous. However, it is worth considering other methods of qualitative data collection. Split interviewing techniques can, for example, be used, involving the telephone, the post and finally the telephone again. (In a business-to-business survey, fax could be used instead of the post.)

The range or extent of information being sought may rule out certain methods. Telephone interviews of over half an hour's duration and self-completion postal questionnaires of many pages can sometimes work, but in general such a length requires face-to-face interviews. In consumer research, in-home rather than street contact is needed for longer interviews.

2. Respondents

The nature of the respondent will have an influence on the selection of an appropriate technique. Some types of respondent cannot be satisfactorily interviewed in particular ways: postal questionnaires are unsuitable if the respondent group has a low level of literacy; street interviewing may not provide adequate coverage of either the elderly or working people (both groups being less likely to be 'on the streets'); telephone interviews are said to be unsuitable for various groups although there is an element of conventional wisdom here. With careful planning, our own company has successfully used the telephone to interview eight-year-old children, dentists at work and managing directors of large companies – all groups said, by some, to be unsuited to telephone coverage.

Fieldwork method may depend on the location of the respondent.

The location of the respondent may affect the selection of the fieldwork method. A programme of face-to-face interviews may be the optimum approach in theory, but a scattered geographical spread may rule out this method on cost or time grounds. The cost of telephone interviews varies far less with distance than face-to-face interviews. Conversely, some respondents are not contactable by telephone, such as site workers and shop-floor workers.

3. Interview requirements

Special requirements of the interview may favour or rule out a particular fieldwork approach. The telephone is clearly not usable if something has to be shown to respondents. However, the telephone in conjunction with a postal survey, or a postal survey alone, is definitely a possibility if only an illustration needs to be shown. It is also possible to mail small products for a placement test. Illustrations (provided there are not too many) and some products can be shown in face-to-face interviews, including those carried out in the street. A requirement to show *and* test products as part of the interview may, however, require a hall, unless a home placement is more appropriate. As already mentioned, long series of scales may be best completed face-to-face or in self-completion questionnaires.

The required level of response may rule out certain methods.

Although a *high* level of response is the ideal in all surveys, a lower level of achievement may be acceptable in the light of the research objectives and the structure of the market covered. A major limitation of postal surveys is the low response rate and this technique could be ruled out in situations where this factor is critical.

4. Resources

The final three factors influencing the choice of fieldwork method are

Consider each of the criteria influencing the selection of research method. Cross out inappropriate methods and circle the optimum for your survey. Finally, rank the criteria to decide what weight you give to the selected methods.

Nature of information
Face-to-face: street, home, work; in-depth; hall/clinic; placement; telephone; postal; telephone/postal split; other

Range of information
Face-to-face: street, home, work; in-depth; hall/clinic; placement; telephone; postal; telephone/postal split; other

Who is to be interviewed
Face-to-face: street, home, work; in-depth; hall/clinic; placement; telephone; postal; telephone/postal split; other

Location of respondents
Face-to-face: street, home, work; in-depth; hall/clinic; placement; telephone; postal; telephone/postal split; other

Special interview requirements
Face-to-face: street, home, work; in-depth; hall/clinic; placement; telephone; postal; telephone/postal split; other

Response rates
Face-to-face: street, home, work; in-depth; hall/clinic; placement; telephone; postal; telephone/postal split; other

Interviewing resources
Face-to-face: street, home, work; in-depth; hall/clinic; placement; telephone; postal; telephone/postal split; other

Timetable
Face-to-face: street, home, work; in-depth; hall/clinic; placement; telephone; postal; telephone/postal split; other

Budget
Face-to-face: street, home, work; in-depth; hall/clinic; placement; telephone; postal; telephone/postal split; other

Figure 3.1 *Checklist for selecting an appropriate method of fieldwork*

different in nature from those previously discussed. They are all concerned with practical constraints and they may result in the use of a method which, on other grounds, is far from ideal.

The availability of resources may constrain the interviewing methods.

Interviewing methods are often constrained by the available resources. Face-to-face interviews are frequently the ideal method of researching the market but with only a small team to do the work, telephone interviews may be the only possible approach. Lone researchers may be limited to a postal survey.

Time can lead to compromises.

Similarly, time can lead to compromises. If the deadline is pressing, only telephone interviews may be practical. (This said, face-to-face interviews can be carried out very quickly given the necessary organisation and budget.) Equally, it is difficult to hurry postal surveys – it can take three to four weeks to get all the returns in from the time of mailing. Although consumer group discussions can be recruited, held and reported on quickly, there are dangers in skimping on the recruitment time. In business-to-business groups, an adequate lead time *must* be allowed.

Budgets may enforce compromises.

Last, but definitely not least, is the constraint of budgets. The ideal research method may just not be affordable and a compromise will have to be made. However, there is a point beyond which it is probably better not to do research at all rather than to carry out grossly inadequate work because funds are not available. Figure 3.1 is a checklist which shows the choice of fieldwork methods.

Sampling and respondent selection

Except in special and rare cases, fieldwork is carried out using a *sample* of the population rather than the whole universe – 500 consumers, say, throughout the country, are interviewed rather than everyone. Without sampling procedures, and confidence that the results obtained in this way are in some way representative of the whole, market research would not be possible.

Questions to be answered when deciding the sample.

When deciding on the sample, you need first to answer these three questions:

- Who should be interviewed in the fieldwork?
- How many of them should there be?
- How should they be chosen?

1. Choosing the respondent

In consumer research, who should be interviewed is sometimes given too little thought. Often, the aim is vaguely to interview consumers who make the decision to purchase a product. This may be a complex issue.

Consider marmalade. In a 'traditional' British family, the marmalade jar is selected in the shop by the housewife and, therefore, the obvious plan is to carry out marmalade research among housewives. However, the housewife's choice may be made to please her own tastes or she may decide on a brand to meet a specific request of her husband or children. She may even buy two brands to cater for various tastes. Depending on the information sought, the people who should be interviewed in this case could include housewives (only), adults (only) or adults and children. Assumptions have to be made about who is involved in the decision (perhaps based on preliminary research). A further complication is that, in practice, the traditional family is no longer the universal consuming unit. Marmalade is also bought by single-person households and other types of household. Even in the traditional family, there are changes in roles, which should be considered.

Carefully consider the assumptions you make when selecting a respondent.

In the 'marmalade' example, we thought about the types of consumer that should be interviewed on the basis that they played some appropriate role in the buying/specification decision. However, there may be other considerations such as:

- Area: do you want to cover a particular region only, the whole country, Western Europe, etc?
- Ownership of or access to particular goods or services: major home improvement product surveys usually cover home owners and not tenants because the latter are unlikely to install, say, central heating in someone else's property.
- Level of income or status: a study of luxury kitchens is likely to exclude respondents below a certain income level.

2. Determining sample error and the size of the sample

A common fallacy when deciding how many respondents to interview – that is, selecting the sample size – is that a particular proportion (10 per cent, 25 per cent, etc.) of the universe should be covered. Forget what proportion should be covered and concentrate on the absolute size of the sample. Generally, the larger the sample, the greater the accuracy, provided it is selected in an appropriate way (see Chapter 6).

Generally, the larger the sample, the greater the accuracy. However, the law of diminishing returns must be considered.

Diminishing returns apply, however, and the increased accuracy from additional interviewing may be very small and not worth paying for.

Statistical theory allows the accuracy of a sample to be calculated within probabilities. An example of an accuracy statement for a random sample of 500 households might be expressed as follows: *10 per cent of the households in our sample had fitted window locks. The sampling error, at 95 per cent probability, is ±2.5 per cent.* This means that we can be confident that there is a 95 out of a 100 chance that, among all households, the proportion who have fitted window locks is between 7.5 per cent (−2.5 per cent) and 12.5 per cent (+2.5 per cent).

Readers with more than a passing interest in sampling should read an introductory text on statistics and learn how to calculate the sampling error mathematically. A rough and ready guide is given in Figure 3.2. To use this chart to calculate the sampling error, we need to know two things:

- The number of people interviewed (the sample size)
- The proportion of respondents giving a particular response

By laying a ruler across the relevant points of the sample result column (for example, 10 per cent) and the sample size column (for example, 500), the sampling error can be read off (about 2.5 per cent). Notice that, as well as varying with the sample size, the sampling error also depends on the sample result, with the greatest error value for a result of 50 per cent. However, you should ponder the implications of indicated errors for a sample of 500 – just under ±1 per cent for a result of 1 per cent compared with about ±4 per cent for a result of 50 per cent. In one case, we are implying a value in the whole population of nearly 0 to 2 per cent and in the other case of a value ranging from 46 per cent to 54 per cent.

The chart in Figure 3.2 can also be used to help choose an appropriate sample size. If we anticipate that a key result will be 50 per cent (for example, proportion buying a particular brand) and that an accuracy of no less than ±2 per cent is acceptable, then the required sample size is approaching 2000. (Try it using the chart.)

This, of course, begs the question: What sampling error *is* acceptable? It is easy to say 'as low as possible', but this ignores the point that increased

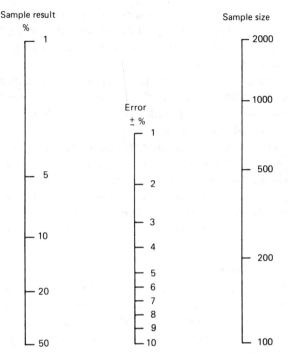

Sample result %

Sample size

Error ± %

Figure 3.2 *Chart for measuring random sampling error (95 per cent probability)*

accuracy has a cost. Furthermore, in practice, a high level of accuracy may not be needed in the context of the decisions that will be taken on the basis of the research. A company considering the potential for improving its sales of a product may accept a broad estimate of the proportion of households having the product (5 to 15 per cent may be quite adequate) but may require much greater precision in a market share estimate (perhaps ±2 per cent).

The level of the sampling error must be considered in the context of the decisions that will be taken on the basis of the research.

In deciding on an appropriate sample size, you may have to consider how large individual *segments* of the sample should be. You may, for example, wish to compare the purchasing levels of three broad age groups – the under 25s, 25–45s and over 45s. This means that you need sufficient respondent numbers to give an adequate level of accuracy for each group. The method used for determining the sample size for the whole sample can also be applied to subgroups.

Some other important points about sampling error and sampling size are:

61

- The level of the sampling error is expressed as a probability only. In the chart, the error levels are shown for 95 per cent probability; this implies a 5 per cent chance that the actual measure in the population is outside the range indicated.
- Strictly speaking, the sampling error calculation only applies when the sample has been drawn randomly. In practice, rather looser sampling methods are often taken as random when considering sampling error and choice of sample size.
- Sampling is by no means the only source of error in a survey and problems such as respondent misunderstanding (or variations in understanding), interviewer mistakes in questioning or recording, data analysis errors (particularly in coding open-ended questions) and problems in drawing the sample can all produce errors greater than the theoretical sampling error.

3. Random sampling

We can now turn to how the sample is chosen. The ideal sample is often regarded as one that is drawn *randomly*. In fact, pure random sampling is very rarely used. It is, however, useful to understand the basic principle of random sampling, if only to recognise the problems in less rigorous approaches.

A random sample of a population (all adults, all households in an area) is one where *each* member of the population has an *equal* chance of being included in the sample. In theory, we could select a random sample by obtaining a list of all members of the population and, starting at a random point on the list, take every 'nth' name where 'n' equals the total number on the list divided by the required sample size. An important condition of random sampling is, therefore, to have an adequate list or sample frame of all members of the population. In practice, this is very rarely available. Clearly, if some individuals are not included in the sample frame, they cannot be selected and this means that bias exists.

In consumer research, the nearest approach to random sampling is the selection of adults from the electoral register. It would be difficult, not to mention uneconomic, to take all the country's registers, treat them as one list and select the sample randomly in one 'run'. Quite apart from the problems of handling a sampling frame of tens of millions, the sample drawn in this way would be spread thinly throughout the country making fieldwork costs horrendous. To overcome such problems, *multi-stage sampling* is usually used. The following example uses a sample of 1000:

1. List all constituencies in the country.
2. Randomly select 10 constituencies (number all, start at a random number and then select at appropriate intervals to yield 10).
3. List all wards within *each* selected constituency and randomly select 10 (using the method outlined in step 2).
4. Take the register of electors for each ward and randomly select 10 individuals (again using a similar method).

The resulting sample from such a multi-stage approach can be interviewed reasonably efficiently (in the example, perhaps by two interviewers per constituency).

Even a sample selected by such a rigorous approach has its problems. Not everyone eligible is included on the electoral registers and such bias could be serious; for example, in a survey to establish the frequency of moving home, it may be important to consider whether individuals moving recently may be missed off the registers.

Consider areas where bias may exist.

An approximation to random sampling, which avoids the labour of selecting individuals from the registers, is the *random walk*. As before, a number of small areas or districts (for example, wards) are randomly picked. Then, for each area or district, an interviewer is given one address as a starting point, from which every '*n*th' home, left or right from the starting point, is chosen, taking alternate left or right turns. Inevitably, the interviewer has to exercise some discretion and there is some danger of uncheckable short-cuts being taken.

Less rigorously, the interviewer might be told to interview any *x* number of homes in the area, each of which must be at least a stated number of doors apart (we are now moving quite a way from a random sample). In any type of household sampling, a decision about which individual within the home should be interviewed must be made and procedures defined to ensure a standard approach.

Random sampling is practical in consumer telephone research (see Figure 3.3). The A–Z directories provide a convenient sampling source and simple procedures can be designed to select individuals. The specific

(1) Make up an acetate template as indicated in the sketch below – the four horizontal lines will be used to pick individuals on each page.

(2) Estimate the number of pages with entries in the directory.

(3) Divide the number of pages by the sample size and multiply this figure by 4 (the number of individuals to be selected per page). This produces the appropriate page interval to select names.

(4) Open the directory at a random page. Lay on the template and list the four individuals closest to the horizontal lines – if the entry is for a business, take the next name below.

(5) Move on according to the page interval and repeat until the sample is complete.

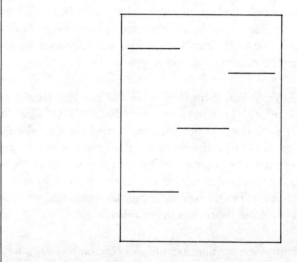

Figure 3.3 *Procedure for selecting a sample from an A–Z telephone book*

directories to be used in a national or regional sample can be selected by procedures similar to those outlined for multi-stage visit sampling.

As a random sample source, telephone books do have limitations:

● Not everyone has a telephone; depending on the subject of the research, it may be decided that this does not matter.

- An increasing proportion of telephone owners are ex-directory and so will be missed from any sample drawn from a telephone book. There is reason to suppose that ex-directory subscribers have some specific characteristics (for example, greater wealth); consequently, their exclusion could introduce bias. However, it is very likely that even if you get through to them, ex-directory subscribers will have low co-operation levels. They may have gone to the trouble of being ex-directory so that they are not bothered by people such as market researchers.
- People who have recently moved will not be in the directory.

Samples drawn from any sort of listing, whether an electoral register or telephone book, are said to be *pre-selected*. This means they have been pre-selected for the interviewer who is allowed no discretion in the matter.

The tedious work of copying names, addresses and telephone numbers for pre-selected samples has to be done, but some benefit can be gained by writing the names on a suitable *contact sheet*. This both assists the interviewer and will later provide a means of analysing response levels. Obviously, not everyone on the sheet will be successfully interviewed, so it is desirable to be able to show the level of successful interviews achieved and the reason for non-response. A contact sheet that you can adapt for your own fieldwork is shown in Table 3.1. It will be seen that the interviewer is expected to attempt contact on up to three occasions.

Show the level of successful interviews and the reason for non-response.

Random sampling, or any approximation to it, is probably of no practical use where a sample of individuals owning, buying or doing something in particular is required. The electoral register, for example, does not indicate whether a household has a video, and this would be a requirement for drawing a sample of video owners. Certainly, we could take a random sample of households, visit them and then interview the video owners, but the wastage and resulting costs of calls on non-owners may be prohibitive.

4. Quota sampling

For better or worse, much consumer market research is carried out by quota rather than random sampling, and this is nearly always the case for street interviewing. The objective of quota sampling is to specify who should be interviewed in terms of critical demographic variables such as

Table 3.1 *Contact sheet*

Job no: _____

Respondent's name	Address	Date/Time of calling			Result	
		1st call	2nd call	3rd call	Successful interview (tick)	Reason for non-interview

Table 3.2 *Quota sheet for sample of 1000 (representative of the UK)*

	Age						
	15–24	25–34	35–44	45–54	55–64	65 +	**Total**
Men	**105** 11%	**94** 9%	**88** 9%	**69** 7%	**65** 7%	**79** 8%	**500** 50%
Women	**93** 9%	**85** 9%	**82** 8%	**65** 7%	**65** 7%	**110** 11%	**500** 50%
Total	**198** 20%	**179** 18%	**170** 17%	**134** 13%	**130** 13%	**189** 19%	**1000** 100%
ABC1	**79** 8%	**72** 7%	**68** 7%	**54** 5%	**52** 5%	**75** 8%	**400** 40%
C2DE	**119** 12%	**107** 11%	**102** 10%	**80** 8%	**78** 8%	**114** 11%	**600** 60%
Total	**198** 20%	**179** 18%	**170** 17%	**134** 13%	**130** 13%	**189** 19%	**1000** 100%

age group, social class and sex. The sample is split into quotas (numbers of people of a certain class) to mirror the population as a whole. Interviewers are then instructed to meet these quotas. They contact respondents until everyone with the 'right' characteristics has been covered. Table 3.2 shows a quota sheet used to select a sample of 1000 adults, representative of the UK in terms of age, social class and sex. The percentage values show the demographics of the population and the numbers in bold show the corresponding sample numbers by 'cell'. Separate sheets might then be prepared for each interviewer; for example, quota sheets for 25 interviews and, therefore, on each such sheet, the 'master' sample numbers are divided by 40.

Regardless of whether the sample is random or quota, the number of respondents included from specific demographic groupings can be small, unless the sample is very large. For example, in the sample shown in the quota sheet, the total number of respondents in the ABC1 class and 65+ is only 75 out of a total of 1000. This is fine unless it is intended to draw conclusions about differences between the groupings within the sample. If this is required, it may be necessary to over-represent some groupings within the sample. In the example, you may increase the

ABC1/65+ cell to 150. The effect of this is to skew the whole sample so that it is no longer representative of the total population. Because, however, the distortion is controlled and known, weighting can be used at the analysis stage to adjust the total sample values in line with what they would have been if the sample had been fully representative. Weighting is also, and less legitimately, used to correct samples that just turn out to be unrepresentative (see Chapter 7 for a further comment on weighting).

Qualitative research also uses quota samples, although of too small a size to be valid in the strict, statistical sense. However, the aim of qualitative research is not to produce numeric measures, so the issue of sample size is, in practice, put on one side.

5. Sampling in business-to-business markets

There are very different problems associated with sampling business-to-business markets. The respondents in this case are representatives of companies or other organisations and are selected because they are believed to influence corporate decisions relevant to a study. In practice, business-to-business surveys often cover respondents with a particular job title, such as 'The Buyer' or 'The Works Manager'. For example, in research to establish attitudes to contract hire of vehicles and providers of this service, it may be decided to interview 'transport managers' or, less specifically, 'the person in charge, day to day, of a company's fleet'. It is very likely, however, that the mode of operating a vehicle fleet may involve a number of decision-makers. These could include:

- The board – which acts as a purchasing committee on large amounts of expenditure
- The finance director – who may have a view on the way the deal should be financed (for example, by outright purchase or contract hire)
- The sales or marketing staff – who may be concerned with the ability of the new trucks to deliver the company's goods reliably and on time
- The transport manager – who may decide the type of vehicle to be acquired
- The drivers – who have to sit in the trucks all day and can wreck models they do not like

It is important to decide what aspect of decision-making must be covered.

In business-to-business research, it is important to decide, as precisely as possible, what aspect of decision-making must be covered. If, in the foregoing example, the key questions concern choice of vehicle make, then the transport manager is the most likely person for interview. However, this does not mean that all interviews will be carried out with the transport manager. Screening questions must be used to ensure that the correct person is contacted. In this case, since our interest is focused on who chooses the make of truck, the fact that others influence or decide other issues is irrelevant (such as whether or not to use contract hire).

The decision-maker often varies widely between different companies, even within an industry, and it may be dangerous to assume in advance that a particular job title should be interviewed. Instead, the choice of who to interview should be made after preliminary screening questions.

Screening must be carried out to ensure that the correct person is interviewed.

Generally speaking, pure random sampling is not used in business-to-business research. It is usually neither practical nor desirable. However, there are exceptions. In researching some service trades, the population can be treated as similar in nature to a population of individuals. Furthermore, there may well be a sampling source, such as a classified trade directory, from which the random sample can be chosen.

In most business-to-business research, however, random sampling is not appropriate. In consumer research, individual respondents can usually be regarded as having equal importance – someone with an annual income in millions may drink more beer than a poor man but the difference in consumption levels will not be in proportion to income. It is very different in the case of companies and other organisations. For example, the energy consumption level of a major car maker is thousands of times greater than that of a small custom car converter, yet both enterprises may be classified and listed as motor manufacturers. A random sample drawn from a listing of companies in the automotive industry could well include very many small enterprises (because most are small) and very few large ones. However, the largest five may well account for over one-half the energy consumption of the whole industry and may be missed entirely. Research to quantify the industry's energy consumption using such a sampling method would produce grossly inaccurate estimates.

Random sampling is not appropriate.

Problems of this sort are usually met through the use of *stratified sampling*. The basic principle is to list, in order of importance, all the units in the sector to be researched. This ranking may be in terms of company size – turnover or number of employees – or the criterion may be directly relevant to the subject of the research. The whole sample is then divided

Stratified sampling.

69

Table 3.3 *Stratified sample of textile industry*

Size of establishment (No of employees)	No of establishments in industry	Percentage to be included in sample	Sample number
Over 5000	132	50	66*
4999–1000	154	25	39
999–100	751	10	75
Under 100	2709	5	135
Total	3646	9	315

* One-half by visit interview; all other fieldwork by telephone

into a number of groups or strata and each is treated separately when deciding on sample size and selection.

An example of a stratified sample of the textile industry is shown in Table 3.3. Using judgement to weight the sample towards the larger firms, a total of 315 establishments were selected for interview. The sample is stratified into four groups depending on the size of the establishment. One-half of all the large establishments but only 5 per cent of the smallest are included.

Stratified sampling requires adequate information on the universe being sampled. You need to know the breakdown of the industry in terms of, say, turnover or employees and, ideally, to have a listing of all companies with the size of each identified. At least in larger industries there are statistics that provide a breakdown of the industry (although they may be some years out of date), but a listing identifying the size of each company is less likely to be available. In this case, the approach is to set interview quotas for each stratum (as in Table 3.3) and then 'find' the companies to meet the quotas. Desk research sources and the opinion of initial respondents should enable the companies in the top stratum to be identified without too much difficulty.

The sample covered must be adequate.

Unlike consumer sampling, business-to-business research inevitably involves judgement to ensure that the sample covered is adequate. Any necessary adjustments can be made to the sample during the fieldwork programme. The data from initial interviews may suggest a need to modify the initial sample list. Questions may be included in the interview to identify leading companies in the field; company executives usually know who their competitors are.

Because of this frequent need for *judgement sampling*, business-to-business fieldwork often needs continuous monitoring in a way that consumer research does not. Where all the interviewing is carried out by a researcher responsible for the whole project, continuous monitoring is easy. Where a team of fieldworkers is involved, it may be desirable to carry out the interviewing in stages and review the results from each before proceeding.

Statistical methods (as in our sample error chart) cannot be used to estimate the accuracy of judgement samples. In any case, the sample sizes typically used in business-to-business research are so small that the sampling errors indicated by this approach would be enormous (look back to the chart in Figure 3.2 to see the sampling errors for a sample of 100 – quite a large sample in business-to-business market research). Any estimate of the accuracy of a judgement sample is usually a qualitative statement based on which individual companies have been included and the nature of the data sought. A carefully selected sample of 100 companies may cover over 80 per cent of the purchasing power in an industry.

In building up samples for business-to-business research, a wide range of sources are usually available for use as *sampling frames*, although they are never complete and up to date. Often, it is desirable to use several sources to build one sample. Some specific types of sample frame are:

Sample frames.

Classified telephone directories and Yellow Pages

All businesses are on the telephone and they get a free entry in the Yellow Pages. They will, therefore, be included somewhere in this source; the difficulty may be to know in which section the group of businesses you are interested in has been classified. Unfortunately, the way a sector is classified to meet the needs of a particular research programme may not be how the directory separates it. Another difficulty is that the directories cover quite small areas, rather than the whole country, making them of limited use for drawing a national sample of a specific type of business.

In practice, classified telephone directories are most useful for researching trades and businesses providing goods and services to the consumer market, and where an approximation to a random sample (rather than stratified) is appropriate.

General directories

These aim to list all companies or units above a certain size and to classify them by industry. Details on the size of individual companies may also be provided. Examples of this sort of directory in the UK are *Kompass* and those published by Dun & Bradstreet.

General directories of this sort are never complete and their coverage varies between industries. They are, however, a very useful general tool and essential for any business-to-business researcher. At a cost, the labour of drawing samples from them can be reduced by having specially tailored print-outs produced by the larger directory publishers. Many can also be ordered through an on-line computer.

Specialised directories

Almost every industry has one or more specialised directories devoted to it. Often, these contain far more information about the companies in the industry than general directories. The *Computer Users Yearbook*, for example, lists establishments with mainframes and provides details of the computer in use; very useful if, for example, there is a need to interview owners of certain models of computer. Directories of this sort may also name decision-makers within companies, providing at least a useful initial contact.

Specialised directories of this sort are so numerous that time needs to be allocated to locating and evaluating those relevant to your own research. Directories of directories are also available to help the search.

The cost of some of the directories can be quite high but others are cheap or even free (see also Chapter 2).

Other sources

There are numerous other sources that can be used as sample frames including:

- *Magazines and journals* which may mention or list companies. Advertising in these publications may also be a source of information.

Decision/behaviour critical to the study

_____

_____

Appropriate respondent:

- Demographic status: _____

- Job title/responsibility: _____

- Ownership/behaviour criteria: _____

Accuracy required ± per cent and why?

_____

Sample size:_____

Sample type:

- Consumer – Random pre-selected ( ) Random walk ( )
  Quota ( ) – to represent _____

- Business-to-business – Stratified ( ) Random ( ) Other ( )

Sample source: _____

Figure 3.4 _Worksheet: sampling checklist_

- _Mailing lists_ sold primarily for direct mail marketing. These rarely make any claims to a high coverage of a sector.
- _Customer lists_ built up by a company. However, they may not include some key companies and are also a biased source.
- _Observation._ In some cases, driving round an area may be the only way to build up a list of certain types of establishment.

Business-to-business samples are generally pre-selected in the sense that they are listed wholly or partly before interviewing starts. Contact sheets (as described earlier) should be used.

The checklist in Figure 3.4 provides a quick reference when planning your own sampling method.

Planning and controlling the fieldwork programme

A successful fieldwork programme requires detailed planning and control in areas other than deciding the appropriate interviewing and sampling methods. Some important areas to plan include the following.

1. Booking an interviewing team

Minimise interviewers' travelling time.

Small-scale interviewing may be best carried out by one researcher. Beyond that, a team of interviewers is required and we will assume that, from your own resources or via an agency, you have access to trained interviewing staff in appropriate areas. Try to minimise the time the team will have to spend travelling to interview points; it is not only travel expenses, but wasted time that has to be paid for.

Generally, it is best to allocate a small number of interviews to each interviewer. This means that the work can be completed more quickly and, if one interviewer lets you down, only a small number of interviews are lost. To allow for such losses, it is also desirable to allocate 5 to 10 per cent more interviews than are actually needed.

2. Briefing interviewers

Some briefing is required for interviewers.

It is no good just sending interviewers a bundle of questionnaires and hoping they will get on with it. They need some sort of briefing. In a complex survey, with a large budget, or where the team is small, a briefing for all interviewers should be held. This is, without doubt, the best method and minimises interviewer misunderstanding or variability in approach. However, in smaller surveys or those that are quite straightforward, written briefing notes are usually sufficient.

3. Questionnaire printing

Printing hundreds of questionnaires takes time as well as money. Both the printing time and cost must be allowed for. To save space and postage costs, double-sided printing is best. Print enough to allow for re-allocation and to have some available for 'office' use. The questionnaire does not have to look beautiful, but it should be clear and easy to follow.

4. Despatch

Mail questionnaires well in advance to allow for mishaps.

In many a survey, questionnaires have disappeared in the post, so this sort of problem should be anticipated. Also, outward and inward despatch takes time. Interviewers are booked to start work on a specific day and will be annoyed, and want paying, if the necessary material is not delivered to them on time. If you delay the mail-out, you may end up using a more expensive method to get the questionnaires 'into the field' on time. It is good practice to ask interviewers to obtain some proof of posting for returned work.

5. Monitoring and chasing up interviewers

Some system is required to control and monitor the despatch of and return of completed questionnaires from each interviewer. You should expect to have to chase up interviewers. Despatch should be started in good time so that it is possible to reallocate work if, for any reason, an interviewer fails to do the work assigned.

6. Quality control and check-backs

On receipt, each quesionnaire should be checked or 'edited', and mistakes in completion or ambiguities flagged and possibly referred back to the interviewer.

It is also good practice to carry out a programme of *check-backs* on some of each interviewer's questionnaires. This is done by selecting a number of questionnaires and recontacting the respondents by visit, telephone or letter. The aim may be simply to establish that the interview is genuine

Carry out a programme of check-backs.

Project: _____		
Project manager: _____		
Required completion date: _____		
Task	**Date required**	**Date completed**
Design/draw sample	_____	_____
Finalise questionnaire	_____	_____
Book interviewing team	_____	_____
Print questionnaire/other material	_____	_____
Despatch to interviewers	_____	_____
(Hold briefing meeting)	_____	_____
Start chase-up	_____	_____
All questionnaires returned	_____	_____
All questionnaires edited	_____	_____
Check-backs started	_____	_____
Check-backs completed	_____	_____

Figure 3.5 *Worksheet: specimen fieldwork planning sheet*

Table 3.4 *Interviewer allocation sheet*

Job no: _____

Interviewer	Area	No of interviews allocated	Date work despatched	Date work expected back	Date received	Notes

(all researchers occasionally come across the made-up interview) or to ask some key questions again and compare the responses with the original questionnaire. Such check-backs validate the quality of the specific job and, where the interviewing team is used continuously, they help to maintain general standards.

A specimen checklist to help you to plan a fieldwork programme and an example of an interviewer allocation and control sheet are provided in Figure 3.5 and Table 3.4 respectively.

CHAPTER 4

QUESTIONNAIRE DESIGN

Questionnaires draw out information for analysis.

Think of a market researcher and you think of a person with a clipboard completing a questionnaire. Questionnaires are a symbol of the work of the market researcher and for good reason. They are the means by which information is sought and recorded in preparation for analysis.

In this chapter, we show how to design questionnaires that really work; that is, ones that draw out the information from respondents accurately and painlessly. First, we consider the role of the questionnaire.

The role of the questionnaire

The questionnaire is a means of structuring the interview so that every person spoken to is asked the same questions.

A questionnaire is a list of questions. Without this list, a market researcher may forget the questions to be asked. Certainly, in a large programme where many interviewers are involved, they would almost certainly all ask the questions in a different manner. The questionnaire is, therefore, a means of structuring the interview in an orderly fashion to ensure that each and every person spoken to is asked the same questions. Usually, but not always, the questionnaire is a form on which to write down the answers. In this capacity, it becomes the vehicle for collating the many responses to show how many people said one thing or the other. Thus, the questionnaire provides the raw material for the data processing.

In summary, a questionnaire:

- Gives order to an interview

- Ensures all questions are asked in the same way
- Is a form for recording data for analysis

Types of questionnaire

Market researchers classify questionnaires according to the degree of discretion they allow the interviewer when administering the questions

Table 4.1 *A classification of questionnaires*

Type of questionnaire	Areas of use of questionnaire	Administration of the questionnaire
Structured	Used in large interview programmes (anything over 50 interviews). Typically used in consumer market research where it is possible to anticipate closely the possible responses.	Street interviewing Home interviews Telephone Self-completion
Semi-structured	Used in business-to-business market research where there is a need to accommodate widely different responses from companies. Also used where the responses cannot be anticipated.	Face-to-face Telephone
Unstructured	Used in depth interviewing of consumers both one-to-one and in groups. Allows probing and searching where a skilled researcher is not fully sure of the responses before the interview. Also widely used in business-to-business market research.	Home interviews Group discussions Industrial visit interviews Depth telephone interviews

(see Table 4.1). A questionnaire that requires the interviewer to stick only to the questions as they are written down is called a *structured* questionnaire. Structured questionnaires are used whenever a large number of interviews are to be carried out, and when it is important that every person is asked the same questions in the same order and the responses are recorded in the same way.

Unstructured questionnaires allow the researcher to modify the interview to suit the circumstances.

The opposite extreme is the *unstructured* questionnaire, which is a checklist of questions used to guide a discussion. The discussion could be an in-depth interview or involve a group of people. The unstructured questionnaire allows the researcher to modify the interview to suit the circumstances but, to do so, skill and experience is required. Furthermore, the findings from the interview will be either written in note form or recorded on tape. It is impractical to analyse many interviews carried out in this way and so unstructured questionnaires are limited to small interview programmes carried out by experienced market researchers.

In the middle ground, between the structured and unstructured questionnaires, are *semi-structured* questionnaires. In a semi-structured questionnaire, there is a loose order of questions and a suggested wording of the questions. Very often, semi-structured questionnaires include open-ended questions, to allow respondents to explain things in their own words. The interviewer is given the authority to adjust the questions to suit a particular circumstance. Semi-structured questionnaires are used widely in business-to-business interview programmes where it is necessary to maintain some flexibility to allow for the wide differences that exist between respondent firms.

Types of question

Just as it is possible to classify types of questionnaire, so too the questions that form them can be classified. There are two ways in which questions can be classified and both are important:

- According to whether the question is *open* or *closed*
- According to whether the question is about *behaviour* or *attitudes*, or for the purposes of *classification*.

A closed question is one where the responses have to be fitted into predefined categories.

1. Open and closed questions

A *closed question* is one where the responses have to be fitted into predefined categories. The simplest of all closed questions is called a 'dichotomous question' – that is, one to which the answer can only be 'yes' or 'no'. (In practice, there are often cases where 'don't know' is a reasonable alternative.) Closed questions are useful to the interviewer because they save time – completing the questions simply involves ticking boxes or circling numbers, as shown in the following:

Q1 Having tasted xxx, how likely or unlikely would you be to buy it?
(Tick relevant answer.)
- Very likely ( )
- Quite likely ( )
- Neither likely nor unlikely ( )
- Not very likely ( )
- Not likely at all ( )

Q2 Including your visit today, how many times have you visited this store in the last month? (Circle relevant answer.)
- Once 1
- Twice 2
- Three times 3
- Four times 4
- Five to six times 5
- Seven to fifteen times 6
- More than fifteen times 7

Closed questions can be prepared for the convenience of the interviewer alone. In these circumstances, the respondent is unaware of the categories of response on the questionnaire. The interviewer uses them as a simplified way of classifying the answer. It saves time writing out what was said, and it saves time and money coding open-ended questions at a later time. If these pre-coded answers to a closed question are not to be declared to the respondent, there should be a warning on the questionnaire for the interviewer not to prompt the respondent.

Equally, there are many occasions when the predetermined response categories are read out to the respondent (in rotation to avoid bias) or they are shown on cards (again, a number of cards may be used in which the order is changed so that there is no bias in the sequence in which they are presented). In such cases, the interviewer should be given clear instructions – for example, 'show prompt card A'. This approach of asking the respondent to choose between a number of predetermined responses guides and aids the thought process.

Sometimes the respondent is allowed to mention some other factor, even though most of the responses are closed. This is to safeguard against the omission of a vital response code at the time the questionnaire was designed.

Open questions are useful for teasing out the subtleties that may not surface in a closed question.

An *open question* is where the respondent is left free to give any answer and this is written down verbatim. Open questions are useful for teasing out the subtleties that may not surface in a closed question. Verbatim responses can be listed at the end of the survey and they can give more insights than can be obtained with a closed response. Just noting the words that people use in answer to a question can be very revealing. It is not always possible to pre-empt an answer and build in the response categories, in which case the researcher has to use an open question. In the following example, note the routing instructions in the answer to the dichotomous question (Q9A). Question 9B was left open ended because the range of possible answers was wide, and if a precoded list of possible responses had been created, it would have been very lengthy.

Q9A Did you receive any help with your attempts to give up smoking?
- Yes 1 GO TO 9B
- No   2 SKIP TO 12

Q9B What help?

_____

_____

_____

Open questions are difficult to analyse in any number – say, anything over 50 to 100. Each open-ended reply has to be considered separately and then grouped together with others of a similar meaning so that a count can be made of how many said one thing or the other. The grouping of open-ended questions is both time consuming and difficult because the answer written on the questionnaire may not make it absolutely clear what the respondent meant – and it is too late to ask for clarification. Making judgements on how to classify the responses is a potential source of error. The following example illustrates some sample verbatim responses made to an open-ended question:

8. And what do you particularly like about the design and shape of this beer bottle?

- 'It is old and traditional, functional. You can see what you get.'
- 'Looks a decent size.'
- 'Don't know, looks nice to see what you are drinking.'
- 'Used to it.'
- 'It's clear and it looks like you can get more in it.'
- 'You can see what you are getting.'
- 'Good size, you can get your hand round it.'
- 'The shape is a bit old fashioned, but normal looking.'
- 'You can see what you are drinking.'
- 'Looks a traditional style bottle.'
- 'Not old fashioned, just what a beer bottle should look like.'
- 'Easy to catch hold of, see what's in it, being clear.'
- 'It's not false looking, it's just a beer bottle.'
- 'Easy to pour out, not let air in.'
- 'Plain.'
- 'Nothing.'
- 'My favourite drink.'
- 'Standard, easy to handle.'
- 'It is clear glass, you can see what is inside, a traditional bottle.'
- 'Easy to hold and drink out of.'
- 'Easy to drink out of.'
- 'More in it, it looks as if it would hold more than the others.'
- 'Simple, uncluttered.'
- 'Glass.'
- 'Because it is clear, simple shape.'
- 'I like the clear glass, the bottle looks like a handy shape.'
- 'Slim, with old bottle neck.'
- 'Looks nice.'
- 'You can see what's in it.'
- 'Plain, simple.'
- 'How fat it goes at the bottom.'

Look through them and gauge the difficulty of deciding the categories that could be used to classify them. Table 4.2 shows the results of the analysis finally achieved from the 31 interviews.

2. Behaviourial, attitudinal and classification questions
Questions can also be classified according to the type of information that is collected, as shown in Table 4.3.

Table 4.2   *Results of bottle design analysis*

Features liked in bottle design	Percentage mentioning feature
Can see the contents	23
Bottle is easy to handle	16
Traditional shape	13
Simple/plain shape	13
Good size	10
Just like the shape	10
Eyecatching/appealing	3
Modern shape	3
Don't know	6
Others (each mentioned once)	29
Total	*

* Multi-response question so total can exceed 100 per cent.

Behaviourial questions

Behavioural questions record facts.

First, there are behaviourial questions. These are questions that seek to find out what people do – for example, whether they go to the cinema, how often they go, where they go, who they go with, etc. They determine people's action in terms of what they have eaten (or drunk), bought, used, visited, seen, read or heard. Behaviourial questions record *facts* and not matters of opinion.

Behaviourial questions address the following:

- Have you ever . . . ?
- Did you ever . . . ?
- When did you last . . . ?
- Which do you do most often . . . ?
- Who does it . . . ?
- How many . . . ?
- Do you have . . . ?
- In what way do you have it . . . ?
- In the future will you . . . ?

For example:

Table 4.3 *A classification of questions*

Type of question	Information sought	Types of survey where used
Behavioural	Factual information on what the respondent is, does or owns. Also, the frequency with which certain actions are carried out. Where people live.	Surveys to find out market size, market shares, awareness, usage rates.
Attitudinal	What people think of something. Their image and ratings of things. Why they do things.	Image and attitude surveys. Brand mapping studies.
Classification	Information that can be used to group respondents to see how they differ one from the other – such as age, gender, social class, location of household, type of house, family composition.	All surveys.

Q1 Do you personally ever buy xxx?
- Yes   ( )
- No   ( )

Q2 How often do you buy xxx?
- At least weekly   ( )
- Between weekly and monthly   ( )
- Between once a month and once every six months   ( )
- Less often than every six months   ( )
- Don't know/can't remember   ( )

Q3 From which types of shop or retail outlet do you buy xxx?
(SHOW PROMPT CARD)
- Chemist/drug store   ( )

- Supermarket/hypermarket ( )
- Corner store/local shop ( )
- Mail order/catalogue ( )
- Home party/neighbour ( )
- Other (state source) ( ) _____

Q4 Which member of your household is mainly responsible for buying xxx?
- Male head of household ( )
- Female head of household ( )
- Children (16 or over) ( )
- Children (under 16) ( )
- Other (specify) ( ) _____

Attitudinal questions

Attitudinal questions seek to find out what people think.

Matters of opinion are collected by the second class of questions – attitudinal questions. As the term suggests, these questions seek to find out what people think of something – how they rate certain films, in what way they think the cinema is better or worse than the television, why they go to the cinema, etc.

Attitudes or opinions are always important in surveys as they are pointers to people's motivations and, therefore, their likely buying habits. Of course, it may be necessary to take other factors into consideration to interpret fully the answer to an attitudinal question. For example, there is not much point asking men what they think of different lipsticks if they never buy them, or seldom influence the colour or type worn by their partners.

It is vital to couch attitudinal questions in a manner that is meaningful to respondents. This could determine the language used in the question, whether it is asked as a verbal rating, a numerical rating or presented as a list of statements where the respondent is asked to agree or disagree. Determining the terminology for attitudinal questions could well involve some depth interviewing before the questionnaire is designed.

- *Verbal rating scales.* Here, respondents are asked to say if they agree or disagree with a statement. It is worth noting that in some cases 'don't know' is a relevant response and provision should be made for it.
- *Numerical rating scales.* This is a very similar approach to the verbal rating except the respondent is asked to give a numerical 'score'

rather than a semantic response. The scores are often out of 5 (where 5 is best and 1 is worst). Ten-point scales are sometimes used but they tend to give responses that are more clustered. A five-point scale fits in well with the five statements ranging from very good to very poor and it yields a distribution of response that has a greater spread, thus enabling researchers to pick out the differences in opinion more easily.

- *The use of adjectives.* A variation on the verbal/semantic scale is to ask respondents which words best describe a product.
- *The use of alternatives.* The respondent is asked to agree or disagree with a number of statements. It is important that the respondent is readily able to identify with one of the statements and not left feeling that in certain circumstances one would apply and in other circumstances the other would be more appropriate.
- *Ranking questions.* A useful way to find out what is most important to a respondent is to present a number of factors and ask which is most important, which is second most important, and so on. Show cards should be used wherever possible to present the factors. However, in order to remove any bias in the order in which they are presented, the factors could each be printed on a different card so that they can be shuffled. If this is likely to prove difficult (for example, in street interviews), the interviewers could have a number of cards on which the factors are presented in a varying order. In ranking questions, it is usually not valid to ask respondents to rank beyond the top three factors. This is because the less important factors become, the more they tend to merge in the minds of the respondents.

Here are some examples of attitudinal questions:

Q1D How *likely* is it in the future that you will try to give up smoking? (SHOW PROMPT CARD D)

Attitudinal questions – some examples.

- Very likely   (   )
- Fairly likely   (   )
- Neither likely nor unlikely   (   )
- Fairly unlikely   (   )
- Very unlikely   (   )

Q1E And if you tried, would you tell me which of these statements best describes the likely result? (SHOW PROMPT CARD E)

- I am sure I would succeed   (   )
- I might succeed   (   )

87

- I'm not sure whether or not I would succeed ( )
- I think I would fail ( )
- I am sure I would fail ( )

Q1F Now, I would like your views on certain aspects of smoking. First of all, would you indicate whether you think that smoking is a major or a minor cause of heart disease by placing a tick in one of the boxes on this scale. (INDICATE HOW TO COMPLETE SCALE)

☐ ☐ ☐ ☐ ☐ ☐
Major cause of heart disease   Minor cause of heart disease

Now, I would like you to fill in the other scales on this page yourself.

☐ ☐ ☐ ☐ ☐ ☐
Major cause of bronchial   Minor cause of bronchial
disorders   disorders

Classification questions

The purpose of classification questions is to group respondents.

The third group of questions is used to *classify* the information once it has been collected. Classification questions are required to analyse the data so that answers from one group of respondents can be compared with those from another. Usually, the information required for a classification question is behaviourial (factual), but since its purpose is to group respondents, researchers tend to treat it differently. Typical classification questions provide a *profile* of the respondents – by finding out their age, sex, social class, where they live, their marital status, the type of house they live in, the number of people in their family, etc.

There are a number of standard classification questions that crop up again and again in market research surveys. These are:

- *Sex.* There can be no classification other than male and female.
- *Household status.* Most researchers classify adults into three groups, which are:
    Head of household ( )
    Housewife ( )
    Other adult ( )
- *Marital status.* This is usually asked by simply saying 'Are you . . .'
    Single ( )
    Married ( )

Widowed   ( )
Divorced   ( )
Separated   ( )

- *Social class.* This is a classification peculiar to UK market researchers whereby respondents are pigeonholed according to the occupation of the head of the household. Thus, it combines the important attributes of income, education and work status. Attempts to move market researchers to classifications according to income group (as is more common in the US) or lifestyle grouping have been slow to catch on. The social class grades that are normally used are in summary:

  A   Higher managerial, administrative or professional
  B   Intermediate managerial, administrative or professional
  C1   Supervisory, clerical, junior administrative or professional
  C2   Skilled manual workers
  D   Semi-skilled and unskilled manual workers
  E   State pensioners, widows, casual and lowest grade workers

  For most practical purposes, the social class groupings are reduced to just four:

  AB ( )
  C1   ( )
  C2   ( )
  DE ( )

  It is not sufficient simply to have boxes (or numbers) on the questionnaire for the interviewers to place a tick to indicate the social class of the respondent. There should be a line to write in the full occupation so that it is possible at a later stage to see that the response is correctly grouped.

- *Industrial occupation.* Researchers may also want to record the type of firm that the respondent works for. In theory, it is possible to classify people according to which slot their company falls into within the Standard Industrial Classification (normally referred to as SIC). Researchers often condense the many divisions of the SIC to suit their convenience. This could be as simple as:

  Primary (farming, forestry, fishing, quarrying, etc) ( )
  Manufacturing ( )
  Retailing and distribution ( )
  Service industries ( )
  Public service ( )
  Armed forces ( )
  Education ( )
  Professions (doctors, dentists, architects, etc) ( )

In a consumer survey, it may be relevant to establish the level of employment of the respondent. For example:

Working full-time (over 30 hours a week)   ( )
Working part-time (8–30 hours a week)   ( )
Housewife (full-time at home)   ( )
Student (full-time)   ( )
Temporarily unemployed (but seeking work)   ( )
Retired   ( )
Permanently unemployed (chronically sick, independent
means, etc)   ( )

The size of the firm in which the respondent works can be important to record, especially in an industrial market research study. Here, the conventional classification is:

0 – 9 employees   ( )
10 – 24 employees   ( )
25 – 99 employees   ( )
100 – 249 employees   ( )
250+ employees   ( )

- *Location.* The location in which the respondent lives is usually recorded. Depending on the scope of the survey, this can be according to standard regions of the UK, ITV reception areas or even a simple split into North, Midlands and South.
- *Neighbourhood.* Recently, there has been a move to group according to the type of neighbourhood in which respondents live. These are often referred to as ACORN or PINPOINT classifications after the market research companies that devised them. They group people into neighbourhood types such as:

Agricultural areas   ( )
Modern family houses, higher incomes   ( )
Older houses of intermediate status   ( )
Poor quality, older terraced housing   ( )
Better-off council estates   ( )
Less well-off council estates   ( )
Poorest council estates   ( )
Multi-racial areas   ( )
High-status, non-family areas   ( )
Affluent suburban housing   ( )
Better-off retirement areas   ( )
Unclassified   ( )

It should be clear from this consideration of classification questions that

B & MR CONSUMER

The Court, High Lane, Stockport SK6 8DX Tel: (0663) 65115

Questionnaire No: _____ No: 28288/C

SMOKERS SURVEY

Classification:

Name: _____

Address: _____

_____

_____

Tel no: _____

Occupation of head of household:

_____

Age of respondent:

15–24	1
25–44	2
45–64	3
64+	4

Sex of respondent:

Male	1
Female	2

Employment of respondent:

Full-time	1
Part-time	2
Unemployed	3
Retired	4
Permanently unable to work	5
Looking after home full-time	6
In full-time education	7
Other	8

Code social class from head of household occupation:

Never worked	0
AB	1
C1	2
C2	3
DE	4

Location:

North	1
Midlands	2
South West	3
South/South East	4
Scotland	5

Figure 4.1 *Typical classification questions*

the researcher can include many different questions in order to analyse and control the sample. However, a cautionary note is necessary since the purpose of the classification questions may not be fully understood by respondents and there can be many refusals to co-operate in answering them. Rather than build in as many classification questions as possible (just in case they could be useful), the researcher should only include those that are really necessary. Apply the *relevance test* first! (See Chapter 1.) A section of a questionnaire covering the classification questions discussed here is shown in Figure 4.1.

General principles of questionnaire design

Think of the objectives of the survey when designing a questionnaire.

When you begin to draft a questionnaire, think of the objectives of the survey – what is it that must be found out? However, while it is important to bear in mind the objectives of the survey, you must not forget the respondent. Questionnaires that fail are those that see questions only from the researcher's point of view. The aim of any questionnaire is to draw out relevant information from respondents as easily and accurately as possible. In order to do this, you should constantly think about the questions as respondents are likely to see them.

1. Keeping the objectives in mind

Every survey has a purpose. Usually, this has been defined on paper and the objectives have been spelt out. Survey objectives can be both general and specific. For example, the global objective of a survey may be to test the effectiveness of an advertising campaign. In order to do this, the researcher must design an interview programme that covers many specific areas of information. It would need to test the awareness of products, the recall of adverts, the buying habits and intentions of the target public, etc. The first step in questionnaire design is, therefore, to write down the objectives of the survey and then list the key subject areas where information is required. To prevent this list from getting out of hand, it is wise to rank the areas of information into those that are essential to the survey and those that are of more peripheral interest.

Imagine that you had to carry out a survey of the type of bread that people buy with the key objective of finding out what share of the market your particular brand held. Think of five key things you feel you want out of the survey and write them down using the specimen worksheet given in Figure 4.2. Now assign an order of priority to each subject. Give serious consideration to whether you really do need to ask those subjects that received a ranking of 4 and 5.

Study name: BREAD SURVEY

Broad purpose of study: To assess the share of my brand within the market

Five key things I have to find out:

What I have to find out	Priority

Figure 4.2 *Worksheet: defining the objectives*

2. Getting a feel for the subject

It is difficult to design a good questionnaire without first becoming steeped in the subject. One of the best ways to do this is to talk about it. If you are to design a questionnaire to find out people's buying habits on hair conditioner, talk about it with your friends. Do they use a conditioner? How often? Who in the family uses the conditioner? Who buys it? Where do they buy it? Do they use a specific brand? What are the benefits of using a conditioner? What are the disadvantages? Such a conversation will help your mind to get into the subject. Points will be raised that you may not have thought about and which need taking into account in the design of the questionnaire.

If the subject to be covered is less general than something like hair conditioner, you will have to seek out a knowledgeable person to speak to. If the survey is about the batteries used in electric fork-lift trucks, speak in the first instance to a buyer or a maintenance man in a factory where electric fork-lift trucks are used. This pre-questionnaire discussion should not be totally without structure. You should have a short list of the subjects to be covered in the questionnaire so that they can guide this preliminary interview. For example, you may have no idea how long fork-lift truck batteries last. Without at least some feel for the length of life of the batteries, it would not be possible to design a question with pre-

Background research is essential if you are to design a meaningful questionnaire.

93

coded responses. One of the discussion points with the respondent at this early stage should be the length of life of the batteries; how variable it is; what affects the length of life, etc. This background is required if you are to design meaningful questions.

3. Drafting the questions

We will assume that the key areas of information required from the study have been listed and some feel for the subject has been obtained by loose discussions with people who buy or use the product. Now begins the task of drafting the questions. Here are four important questions you should ask yourself when drafting a question:

- Will this question be understood in the way that I intended?
- How many different ways could this question be interpreted?
- Is this question likely to annoy or offend?
- Is there a better way of asking the question?

The meaning of questions should be clear straight away.

Don't expect the draft of a question to be right first time. Think about the way questions are posed in ordinary conversation; you often need to obtain further clarification of what was intended by the question. In a market research study involving many interviews, there is no scope for debate about what was really meant in either the question or the answer. The meaning of the question needs to be clear straight away.

4. Things you should take account of when designing a questionnaire

Outline the aim of the questionnaire.

- Write an introduction for the questionnaire. This is to give the respondents some explanation of why it is being carried out. Give assurances of confidentiality and that there will be no follow-up sales pressure (assuming that these assurances can be honestly given).

Ease the respondent into answering the questionnaire.

- Begin with easy questions and those that are less sensitive, so that the respondents are eased into their task.
- Break the interview into topics, so that there is a sensible grouping of questions. This will help the flow and make it easier for respondents.
- Use screening questions to find out if respondents should be asked more questions or if they can skip a few. It is important to use screening questions at the beginning of a questionnaire, as they eliminate people whose views are not required.

Be specific.

- Make all the questions very specific. Be as clear as possible. Usually, this means that the questions should be short. However, there are occasions when it is advisable to lengthen the question by adding memory cues, such as: 'Have you, yourself, bought any xxx in the last three months; I mean in September, October or November?' The memory cue is the listing of the three months.

- If a question looks as if it is becoming too complicated, it may be because it justifies being split into two separate questions.

  Keep questions simple.

- Use words that respondents will be sure to understand. Avoid jargon but be prepared to use colloquialisms if they are more meaningful. In some areas of the North of England, it may be necessary to refer to bread rolls as 'baps' – that being the normal terminology.

  Avoid jargon.

- When referring to a time period, be specific. For example, don't be vague about 'last year' – spell out whether you mean the last 12 months or the last full year from January to December. Remember that there is a temptation for people to extend periods rather than contract them. Pinning down the dates reduces the chances of 'over-claiming' in the responses.

- Vary the types of question. Questions that are all the same cause respondents to get in a groove. In any case, they can lead to boredom or irritability and neither results in quality responses.

  Vary the type of question.

5. Pitfalls to avoid in questionnaire design

Sometimes questions are difficult to answer because the rules of questionnaire design are broken. The pitfalls of questionnaire design are:

- Don't make the questionnaire too long. There is no categorical rule about how long an interview should take. Everything depends on the interest the respondent has in the subject, the place where the interview is taking place and other time pressures to which the respondent may be subjected. In telephone interviews, a maximum of 10 minutes should be aimed for (it is possible to hold people for half an hour but this is seldom good practice). In the street, 10 minutes is also a reasonable maximum given that most people who are stopped will want to go about their business. At home, an interview could take 20 minutes to an hour, depending on the circumstances and its complexity. However, be warned. Long and tedious questionnaires lead to respondent fatigue and a decline in the quality of response towards the back end of the interview.

  Don't make the questionnaire too long.

- Don't make the questions too long or complicated. Included in this common pitfall is the use of a lot of meaningful words in a short space. Beware also of questions that include several ideas and those that have more than one instruction built into them.

- Don't use words that the respondent would not understand or could misinterpret. Jargon that the researcher uses as a shorthand is likely to be a mumbo-jumbo to the respondent. Long words and unusual words are also worth avoiding.
- Don't ask for information that is unreasonable and which may force the respondent to guess. If a person has not used a product for a long time, he may not be able to remember anything about the purchase. Also, asking image questions about a product or a company that the respondent has little knowledge of may produce a reply, but not a meaningful one.

Avoid loaded questions.

- Don't lead the respondent into an answer with a 'loaded' question. Asking respondents if they agree that a product is nice is likely to encourage a positive response.
- Be careful of the word 'you' as it can be confusing. It may not be clear whether the question refers to 'you personally' or 'you and your family'. It is always better to qualify exactly what is meant in the question: 'How much milk did you personally drink yesterday – I mean either on its own, with cereal, or in tea or coffee?'

6. Fine tuning the questionnaire

Once the first draft of the questionnaire has been produced, the researcher needs to read it through again and again, bearing in mind the principles we have just discussed. The aim is to refine the questions by:

- Eliminating ambiguities
- Removing questions that are superfluous
- Adding questions that are needed
- Changing the order of the questionnaire to improve the flow

Reading the questions out loud can be better than going over them in your head. Unless the questionnaire is for self-completion, the questions will ultimately be read out, and so speaking out loud will show what they will really sound like.

The questionnaire must be tested informally before being used in the field.

Once you have made all obvious changes, the questionnaire must be tested, before it actually goes 'into the field'. A good test is to try it out on a colleague or friend. Now is the opportunity to look out for the problems that could occur later. If possible, the dummy run should be carried out without interruption, with you writing in the answers. Timing the length of the interview will give you a guide to how many interviews a day can be carried out (although, clearly, the time taken to find respondents who qualify for interview will also have a major influence on the number that can be completed in a day).

After the interview has been carried out, a post-mortem on each question is required. The guinea-pig respondent should be asked:

- 'What did that question really mean to you?'
- 'What was in your mind when you were answering that question?'
- 'Was there another answer you could have given to that question?'
- 'How would you have asked the question?'

These questions will flush out any weaknesses in the questionnaire in terms of either the meaning of the questions, the length of the questionnaire or its flow.

7. Organising the layout of the questionnaire

Questionnaires are not simply a list of questions, they are also a recording medium for answers. They need to work for the interviewers as well as the respondents. The important rules to bear in mind when arranging the layout of a questionnaire are:

- Give the questionnaire a title at the top of the first page. In a market research agency where many surveys are taking place, it may be necessary to identify the project with a job number on the questionnaire.
- Provide an introduction at the beginning of the questionnaire – something the interviewer can read to the respondent to explain why the survey is being carried out.
- The classification questions can go at the front or the back of the questionnaire. In consumer research, the respondent's name and address are sometimes asked at the end of the interview, so space for this may be left at the end of the questionnaire. Conversely, in industrial surveys, the name of the respondent is established at the beginning of the interview, so space for these details is provided at the top of the first page. Space should also be left at the beginning for the date the interview took place.
- Number all questions clearly.
- Many researchers prefer to design questions where the interviewer indicates the response by circling a number rather than ticking a box. The numbers correspond to the numbers punched into the computer at the time of data analysis and for this reason it makes the data processing task easier.

Circling response numbers rather than ticking boxes can make data processing easier.

97

- Differentiate in some way the questions that should be read out to the respondent and the instructions to the interviewer. Interviewer instructions are often identified by being in capitals or in bold.
- Think about the conditions in which the interview will be carried out. If it is likely to be on a doorstep in winter, make sure that the typestyle is clear and large enough to read in poor light.

Leave enough space for responses.

- Don't cramp the questions. Interviewers like lots of space. Leave sufficient space to accommodate the largest and boldest handwriting.
- In a large-scale survey, where coding will be carried out at a later date, it is useful to have a right-hand margin in which the coders can write their numbers. The margin can also be used to highlight routing instructions such as 'now skip to Q6B'.

Clearly identify the instructions to the interviewer.

- Make sure that the instructions to skip questions are correct. (It is easy to get out of synchronisation with routing instructions; questions will have been added and some taken away in the redrafting process.)
- It can be helpful to have 'flagging statements' at appropriate junctures of the questionnaire to tell the interviewer what the next grouping of questions is about.
- Leave ample space for open-ended questions. (This will vary. In some cases, one line will be enough while in others, half-a-dozen lines may be necessary.) Make sure there is sufficient distance between the lines for the interviewer's bold and hurried scrawl.

Ensure that answers clearly correspond to questions.

- In pre-coded questions, ensure that the boxes (or brackets or numbers) to be ticked are close to the response categories. If they are too far away, there is a danger that the interviewer will misjudge which box belongs to which line and enter the response incorrectly.
- At the end of the questionnaire, include a 'thank you' statement.
- Invest in good printing or photocopying of the questionnaires and use at least 60 gramme paper. Have the questionnaires stapled in the top left-hand corner.

8. Pilot testing the questionnaire

Running the questionnaire past a colleague is not sufficient to iron out the bugs. A real test is required and this should be arranged with real respondents – the type of respondents who will be interviewed when the survey takes place. If the questionnaire is to be administered over the telephone or in the street, the test should be carried out using that medium.

It can be a salutary lesson for whoever designed the questionnaire to hold the clipboard and carry out the first few interviews. There is no finer way of learning if the questionnaire works. It is a bit like forcing architects to live in the buildings they have designed. If the questionnaire is too long, if the questions are not sharp enough, if the questions annoy respondents, if there is insufficient space to write the answers, it will quickly become apparent.

The aim of pilot testing a questionnaire is to make sure that it works. Usually, 20 or so interviews with a cross-section of respondents is all that is necessary to determine if any changes are required. Sometimes as few as 10 pilot interviews are sufficient. Of course, in a survey of industrial buyers or specifiers, piloting may be inappropriate anyway. Industrial companies are all so very different that a response from one may in no way reflect the pattern of response of the others. However, the samples in industrial surveys are generally much smaller than in consumer studies and the researcher often has the flexibility to amend and alter the questionnaire as the interviewing proceeds. Thus, the first few interviews in the survey are closely scrutinised and act as the pilot.

A pilot test of real respondents is needed to ensure that the questionnaire works.

Rules for designing special types of questionnaire

1. Unstructured questionnaires

The rules and guidelines outlined so far are all relevant to structured or semi-structured questionnaires: the type used in street or household interviews. There are, however, a number of special types of interview that require a modified approach to questionnaire design. The first of these is the unstructured questionnaire, used for depth interviews or to steer group discussions.

It is probably more appropriate to think of the interview guided by an unstructured questionnaire as a discussion; that is, the interviewer is exploring and giving consideration to the matter, probably because the boundaries of the subject are not precisely known. This happens frequently in business-to-business studies where the researchers cannot be expected to be knowledgeable about the subject. The first step is to construct a list of topics that shed light on the subject. The aim of this is to provide information that will be a useful input into the survey or will help in designing a more structured questionnaire. The following example will illustrate this.

A company with a large overseas business in cleaning chemicals wanted to enter the UK market but was unsure how to do so. First, it needed to

Explain purpose of the survey. The study is for a company that has an overseas interest in cleaning chemicals and is looking for some form of partnership in the UK. Cleaning chemicals are those used for:

- Ware washing – both sink and dishwasher, including pre-soaks, rinsing agents, 'sparklers', solid and liquid detergents.
- Hard-surface cleaning – including bowl cleaners and sanitary ware de-scalers. It is important within this group of products to distinguish between *food* surfaces and *non-food* surfaces.
- Disinfectant and odour control – both de-odourisers and re-odourisers.
- Drain cleaners – including caustics/alkalines, biological products, etc.
- Laundry products – including powders and liquids, spot and stain removers.

Introduction/background

(1) Nature of company's business. Main and subsidiary businesses. Parent company. Commitment to cleaning chemicals within the group.

(2) History of development of company's business in cleaning chemicals.

Nature of respondent's business in cleaning chemicals

(3) Cleaning products marketed by company. Key products in the range. Any unique products within the range. Products made by company. Whether there is a technology in-house or does the company just mix a concentrate.

(4) Brands sold by company. Involvement of company in own branding. Proportion of company's turnover made by someone else – who makes it. Proportion of company's turnover made for someone else – who this is made for.

(5) Company's total turnover in all products. Company's home and export turnover in cleaning chemicals. Breakdown of turnover by product group. Breakdown of turnover by market segment.

(6) Methods of marketing employed by company. Size of sales-force; use of agents (see point 7); number of distributors; promotional spend on branding/marketing.

(7) Use of agents. Number of agents used. Whether agents have exclusivity on products or geography.

(8) Whether it has its customers tied up on contract. Whether the company has service engineers for any machines.

(9) Company's pricing policy.

Figure 4.3 *Overview checklist for cleaning chemicals survey*

know more about the UK market, but it also needed to know the reactions of possible partners to some form of deal. The researchers were required to assess the size of the market, to describe its prospects and to hold preliminary discussions with UK cleaning chemical companies to establish if they had any interest in a deal. A checklist was devised, which ran to four pages. The first page is shown in Figure 4.3. It will be noted that the researcher who designed the checklist wrote the topics simply as 'memory joggers', to remind him which subjects had to be discussed. The formulation of the precise questions actually took place during the interview itself. It is also worth noting that many of the topics were ambitious; for example, asking cleaning chemical manufacturers to divulge their turnover and to break it down into the different product groups they sell. However, the researcher was working on the age-old principle of all market researchers; that is, 'if you don't ask, you don't get.' No doubt, he would get some useful information from some people, even though others may refuse.

The rules for designing checklists of questions are, therefore:

- It may be useful to include a 'header' that says what the study is about. The researcher can refer to this at the beginning of the interview as the subject is introduced.
- Be comprehensive and ambitious in the subject coverage. List all the subjects you are interested in covering and go for it. The depth interview gives scope to dig deep. **Be ambitious in the questions you ask.**
- The questions or topics are reminders to the interviewer and do not represent the final wording of the question. List the topics as cryptic questions or statements.
- Start with subjects that are fairly broad, working towards those that are more specific. (This is a general principle of questionnaire design that applies to structured questionnaires as well.)
- Use plenty of probes and keep asking the questions: 'Why did you say that?' or 'Can you explain?' **Use plenty of probes.**
- Separate the checklist into subheadings so that you can quickly find your place when the checklist is referred to during the interview.
- Usually, the notes made during the discussion are written on another piece of paper. The checklist is not a form with boxes to tick or lines to write on. It is useful, therefore, if the topics on the checklist have numbers against them so that you can later consult the checklist and see which question the answer referred to.

2. Telephone questionnaires

Questionnaires for distance interviews.

The questionnaires discussed so far have assumed that the interviewer has face-to-face contact with the respondent. This contact allows the interviewer and the respondent to discuss a subject in depth (more so in the home than in the street). In addition, the interviewer can observe the respondent's body language and pick up clues. In face-to-face interviews, it is possible to show cards to the respondent, containing prompts such as brand names, scales, logos or adverts.

Increasingly, the telephone is used as an alternative to face-to-face interviews. The telephone allows speedy, inexpensive access into most homes around the country. However, besides being a communication device, the telephone is a barrier. The respondent and the interviewer never meet. Different interviewing skills are required by the telephone interviewer from those employed in a face-to-face situation and the questionnaire needs special care.

- Time is precious on the telephone – it is not so much the cost of the call (although this can be expensive), rather the difficulty of 'holding' people for more than a few minutes. Because time is a barrier, the questionnaire must be succinct. A 10-minute telephone interview is the maximum that researchers should aim to carry out, although in exceptional circumstances it could go on longer.
- The introduction to the telephone interview needs special attention. It should be communicated quickly and should explain who the interviewer is, the company for which the research is being carried out and what the survey is about. It must be appreciated that the respondent will not be expecting the call and, therefore, will not fully take in this introduction. It is usually courteous to finish the interview by repeating who has done the interview and what it will be used for.
- The interviewer's voice is the sole means of communication on the telephone. Lines may not always be crystal clear. In all questionnaires, it is important to use simple, straightforward English but it is doubly necessary over the telephone. Long words and those with more than one meaning can easily become corrupted by telephone transmission.
- It is not advisable to expect people to be able to answer questions that involve reading out a long list of features. They will not be remembered. Nor is it realistic to ask the respondent to take a pen and write them down at the other end. The use of scales and lists should be kept to a minimum in telephone interviews.

Keep the use of scales and lists to a minimum in telephone interviews.

- Although an obvious point, the telephone precludes the use of visual prompts, and this could prohibit its use for testing packs, adverts or anything that requires sight, touch or smell.
- It is easier to obtain facts over the telephone than to establish attitudes. Getting people to explain things, without being able to witness their gesticulations, can be difficult.
- The telephone spares the respondent's blushes if questions are on a sensitive subject. However, in a 10-minute telephone call, there is not usually enough time to build the confidence and rapport required for in-depth interviewing. Also, the respondent may be inhibited by circumstances at his end, therefore preventing a truthful answer. (Another member of the household listening to one side of the conversation could put pressure on the respondent.)
- A smooth flow in questioning is particularly important on the telephone. Interruptions caused while the interviewer skips between questions or switches from one subject to another can lose the interest and concentration of the respondent.

A smooth flow in questioning is particularly important on the telephone.

3. Self-completion questionnaires

Self-completion questionnaires require the respondent to read the questions and fill in the answers. They can be a tempting method of data collection if you are working alone, as it is possible for one person to send out large numbers of questionnaires. There are no problems of organising and briefing the interviewers as in face-to-face or telephone surveys. However, most respondents have an aversion to self-completion questionnaires, which may be seen as 'just another form'. Response rates are often very low; this is due, in part, to the difficulty of interesting and motivating people to complete them.

Self-completion quesionnaires are one of the most difficult to design. They have to be exactly right as there is no interviewer present to cope with any difficulties the respondent faces in understanding or interpreting the questions. They have to be simple to complete, otherwise the response rate will be very low. They are hard to test because it is difficult to organise the printing and mailing of small numbers for a pilot run. Also, if there is a tight deadline on the whole project, there may be insufficient time for the pilot responses to be returned.

Despite the problems associated with self-completion questionnaires, they do have their place in market research. They yield high returns from new car buyers. They can be easily included in packs of products for the user to complete and return. There are circumstances in a face-to-face interview when it is easier to ask the respondent to self-complete rather than to read out the questions. For example, self-completion is appropriate if the questionnaire includes a high proportion of scalar questions, which would be tedious to answer if they were read out one at a time. By looking at them, the respondent can quickly work through, ticking the boxes himself.

General rules to bear in mind in the design of self-completion questionnaires are:

Keep the layout as well as the questions simple. Closed, dichotomous and scalar questions are ideal for self-completion questionnaires.

- Leave nothing to chance. Instructions have to be absolutely clear, not only those that show how to complete the questions, but also those that specify how to return the questionnaire.
- Try not to have too many routing questions – that is, those that instruct the respondent to skip from one question to another. These are a complication and a source of respondent error.
- Wherever possible, use closed questions. Open-ended questions require the respondent to write in a response and the results are invariably poor.
- Dichotomous questions (to which the answer is either yes or no) are ideal for self-completion questionnaires because they are simple. So too are scalar questions.
- Avoid asking the respondent to complete complex grids. Instead, think of splitting the question up into separate but more manageable parts.
- Spend time (and probably money) getting the questionnaire to look good. Have it laid out well by a printer or use a desk-top publishing package. Print the questionnaire on good paper.
- Don't have the questions packed tightly together.
- Respondents find it easier to tick boxes rather than to circle numbers. However, it may be useful to the data processors to have a small, discreet number tucked away just outside the box.
- Try to restrict the questionnaire to about 30 questions or four sides of A4.
- Design a cover letter that explains exactly what is required of the respondent. The letter should say what the research is about, why the respondent will benefit from completing it and how the questionnaire should be returned. The more the cover letter is personalised, the better – matching in the name of the respondent at the top of the letter and adding a personal signature all helps.

4. Recruitment questionnaires

Market researchers often need to recruit people. Respondents may be asked to attend a group discussion, to visit a market research 'clinic', to attend a hall test or to become a member of a panel of people who are to answer questions over a period of time. The recruitment process is one of taking people through a series of *qualifying* questions until it is determined that they fit the type of person wanted for the study. At that time, the questions are stopped and the persuasion begins, as the interviewer attempts to commit the person to take some further action to help the survey programme.

A questionnaire is used for recruitment purposes because the researchers are always looking for certain types of people and not just anybody. The questionnaire is the logical way to find out if a person fits the survey requirements. Usually, there are quite a few different types of people required to attend group discussions, hall tests, etc., and a quota is set, which states how many of each type should attend.

Special rules for designing recruitment questionnaires are:

- There should be clear instructions to the interviewer on the questionnaire. It is not sufficient to tell the interviewers what is needed at a briefing and assume that they will remember what has been said.
- When carrying out face-to-face interviews, it is best both to read out *and* show a card with the prompts. In so doing, there is less chance of error.
- Recruitment questionnaires work by eliminating people who are not suitable for the research. For example, one of the first questions on a recruitment questionnaire asking people to take part in testing the packaging of frozen foods might be to ensure that the respondents do not work in an occupation that would make their responses biased. Thus, market researchers and people involved in food manufacturing/retailing are eliminated at an early stage.

  Recruitment questionnaires eliminate people who are not suitable for the research.

- The process of elimination goes on so that, eventually, only people who comply with pre-set criteria are asked to the hall test, group or whatever. In the case of the frozen food packaging survey, the questions may concern the packaging of blackcurrant cheesecake or cream scones. If the respondents would never consider eating these delicacies, there is little point seeking their opinion on them.
- The recruitment questionnaire needs to include all the demographic

data appropriate to the survey. Normally, this would include social class, age and gender, but there may well be other classifications besides (number of people in the family, location of dwelling, age of dwelling, etc.). The classification questions depend very much on the subject of the study. A survey on DIY products would need to know the age of the person's home, whereas a survey of food products would require details on the composition of the family.

Give a realistic indication of the commitment needed to help in the survey.

● It is important that the respondent is given some indication of the time that will be taken up by helping in the survey. Besides being dishonest, it only leads to problems to say that their involvement will be for just a few minutes when in fact it will take half an hour.

5. Business-to-business questionnaires

Buyers and specifiers in industry can be interviewed face to face, by telephone or using a self-completion questionnaire. Face-to-face and telephone interviews are by far the most common methods.

A business-to-business questionnaire needs to accommodate responses from a range of respondents.

Business-to-business respondents differ from those in consumer markets in that they are answering questions on behalf of the organisation they represent. The goods and services they buy are not for the individual's personal consumption. The range of responses in business-to-business research is far wider than in consumer markets. A market researcher thinking of interviewing buyers of stationery goods needs to accommodate responses that could range from a buyer at a government department or a public utility through to a small company operating out of a single office. The buyers of stationery at these outlets will buy on a different scale and will be motivated by different factors. This must be accounted for in the questionnaire.

The wide assortment of types and sizes of business means that it is impossible to design a questionnaire that is suitable for each and every one. Questionnaires used in business-to-business market research have to be more flexible. This is not an excuse for lackadaisical questionnaire design. Quite the opposite. The business-to-business questionnaire needs to take account of the special circumstances of all manner of respondents. Some general rules in the construction of business-to-business questionnaires are:

● Allow space for the name and address of the respondent at the top of the questionnaire. One of the first things the interviewer must find out is the name and position of the respondent. In business-to-business market research, it is vital that the interview is carried out with exactly the right person – that is, the buyer or the specifier of the product/service.

- Be prepared to use more open-ended questions in order to gain the flexibility of response that is required. Open-ended questioning allows the respondent to say what is appropriate for him and does not force the responses into categories that are not quite right.

  Open-ended questions will enable more flexibility in the response.

- Business-to-business market research interviews are more akin to discussions. The questionnaire should be written in a discussive/ conversational style. This can, on occasions, mean leading the respondent with statements such as 'Would it be true to say that . . .?' or 'Some people we have spoken to have said . . . . What do you think of that?' Of course, this type of interviewing requires great skill because it aims to open up the discussion, but this is at the risk of biasing the response.

- The business-to-business respondent in industry is more likely than his consumer counterpart to want to know why the research is being carried out and for whom. Instructions as to what can be disclosed on these issues should be given in the questionnaire.

- Most business-to-business respondents are educated people and can cope with sophisticated questions. Any questions that are patronising or agonisingly simple will annoy the respondent.

- Forcing answers into scales or pre-codes can annoy industrial respondents because the pre-codes may not always be an appropriate 'home' for their response. There may not be a simple answer.

CHAPTER 5

CARRYING OUT AN INTERVIEW PROGRAMME

The foundation of market research is interviewing. It is the means by which information is obtained for most surveys. An interview in market research terms is a formal affair in that it is set up by the researcher with a person who has been identified as a source of useful information. Of course, the interview itself may appear very relaxed and the respondent may even see it as a discussion or conversation. However, the interview has a purpose and a closely defined objective. The interviewer's aim is to draw out of the respondent accurate facts and opinion, guided by a questionnaire or checklist.

Interviewers always require respondents to speak honestly and almost always they ask them to give their time freely. Persuading people to do this is not always easy and in this chapter we show how the right approach will encourage co-operation. Keeping good records is an important part of an interviewer's job and we suggest systems that will help in the organisation of a fieldwork programme. Finally, and in contrast to the use of the telephone and face-to-face interviews, we describe how to run a postal research campaign.

Pre-interview planning

Decide how many interviewers are required.

1. Booking interviews
Throughout this chapter, we will assume that the researcher has decided what size of sample is required and what method of data collection is to be used (see Chapter 3). Decisions may still have to be made about how

many interviewers are needed. Indeed, getting hold of the appropriate number of interviewers to do the job may be a problem in its own right.

The number of interviewers needed will depend on whether there are any difficult quotas that must be achieved and, in industrial surveys, the degree to which the respondents have been over-researched in the recent past. Table 5.1 provides some suggestions for the number of interviews that can be achieved daily by different methods.

Table 5.1 *Number of interviews per day according to survey method*

Type of survey	Number of interviews per day
Consumer interviews	
Simple 5-minute street interview	20 – 40
20–30-minute household interview	5 – 15
Simple 5-minute telephone interview	15 – 25
Business-to-business interviews	
30–60-minute face-to-face interview	2 – 4
10–15-minute telephone interview	5 – 15

If you need a ready-made team of interviewers, it may be worth using the services of a *fieldwork agency*. This is a company specialising in the supply of interviewers for market research projects, which charges a rate per interview. The fieldwork agency will be able to advise you on the number of interviews that can be achieved in a day and, on this basis, will offer a price per interview for carrying out the work.

Fieldwork agencies can provide a ready-made team of interviewers.

You can decide if 'interview only' or 'field and tab' (fieldwork and tabulation) is required. In an 'interview-only' project, the agency's contract is simply to deliver the appropriate number of completed questionnaires. In the case of 'field and tab', the agency carries out the interviews, processes them and supplies a computer analysis of the results. The Market Research Society publishes a *Yearbook* in which you can look up the names of fieldwork-only agencies.

There is a big difference in the organisational requirements of a survey involving a number of interviewers and one where you do all the interviewing yourself. In the latter case, you could be working on a study using group discussions or, if it is an industrial project, the method could involve a small number of depth interviews with key respondents. For now, we will consider the problems associated with studies involving a large number of interviews and many interviewers.

In most consumer market research surveys and in many business-to-business surveys, a team of interviewers carries out the fieldwork. At the earliest opportunity, the interviewers need to be booked for the appropriate number of days they will be working. (You cannot expect to be able to find a team of 10 interviewers, each required to carry out 20 interviews, within a couple of days in the middle of May when fieldwork agencies tend to be very busy.) Once booked, the interviewers must be briefed.

2. Briefing interviewers

All interviewers should be briefed.

A briefing is the occasion when the interviewers are told what is required of them, and they are introduced to the questionnaire they will be using and shown how to administer it. Wherever possible, you should brief the interviewers personally. In a market research agency, the job of getting the interviewers together at a suitable venue is the responsibility of the fieldwork supervisor/controller. As it is highly inconvenient if just one interviewer cannot attend a briefing, at least a week's notice (and preferably a couple of weeks) should be allowed for booking the interviewers for the briefing session. The interviewers will have to be paid for their time and the expenses they have incurred travelling to the briefing – a cost that obviously has to be catered for within the overall budget for the project.

At the briefing, you should aim to cover the following subjects:

Interviewers need to be told what is expected of them.

- The overall goal of the study should be stated (or, if the detailed objectives cannot be revealed, you should at least give some general context which makes sense to the interviewers).
- The questionnaire should be fully explained. This involves going through the questionnaire, question by question, so the interviewers fully understand it and know what is intended. It may be necessary to give the interviewers advice on the completion of certain types of questions: complicated grids need to be explained; guidelines on how much to write down on open-ended questions should be given. Interviewers will be interested to know how long the interview is

expected to take and some guideline should be given.

- Special attention needs to be drawn to interviewer instructions on the questionnaire. These include 'routings' (instructions that tell the interviewer to skip questions), when to prompt and not to prompt, when to show cards, when to rotate lists that are to be read out, and so on. Even though all these instructions will be written on the questionnaire, the briefing gives you the opportunity to emphasise *verbally* what the questions are aiming to achieve.

  Explain how to use the questionnaire in full.

- The interviewers must be told where and how to carry out the interviews. If they are to be carried out in the street, the interviewers may need to know where they can and cannot stand. For example, in a survey that seeks to find out which brands of bread people buy, it would bias the results if interviewers stood outside bakers. If the interviews are to take place in the home, the interviewers may have to find people of a certain age or social class against a quota instruction, or they could be given preselected addresses, or there could be a random sampling method that needs explaining.

  Explain where and how to carry out the interviews.

- Call-back policies must be spelt out. In a household survey, it is normal for the interview to be attempted up to three times. Interviewers should be familiar with the guidelines on call-backs. It is also worth stressing that they should be on different days and at different times. There may be other points of detail that could be made at the briefing, such as not to interview after certain hours, not to interview on Sundays, etc.

- Interviewers should be told exactly who to interview. Most surveys are carried out against a quota. A quota is a numerical mix of different types of people to interview. It is often expressed as a certain number of men and a certain number of women (this is known as parallel quota). In the same way, the quota may require a certain number of people in specified age groups and a certain number in social class groupings. If the quota numbers demand that an *exact* number of people should be interviewed who are in a certain age *and* a certain social class grouping, this is known as an interlocking quota (see page 67).

  Interviewers should be told exactly who to interview.

- Interviewers should be given the names of researchers they can contact if they need advice or get into difficulties. Usually, this will be the fieldforce supervisor (or area supervisor) who booked them for the work, but it is also useful for the interviewers to know the name of the researcher controlling the survey and the telephone number at head office.

  Interviewers should be given the names of researchers they can contact if they need advice.

- It is most important to give the interviewers precise instructions on the date for completing the work and how to return the completed questionnaires. Sometimes the questionnaires are collected by area supervisors but more often they are returned through the post. Interviewers should, at the very least, obtain 'proof of posting' so that disputes do not arise about paying for work which, it is claimed, has got lost in the post. The postal system seems to treat all large brown envelopes as parcel post, despite the denomination of stamps, so the words 'FIRST CLASS POST' should be written in capitals. It is usually safer for the questionnaires to be returned to head office by Special Delivery or Recorded Delivery. These are tried and tested systems which seem to get the questionnaires back more quickly (even though the Post Office claims that it makes no difference).

Although the purpose of the briefing is to state verbally what is wanted from the survey, it is also good practice to leave the interviewers with a written summary. This should not be too long, as it would never be read. As a maximum, it should be two pages in length and cover only the important issues.

Sometimes it is neither practical nor necessary to hold personal briefings of interviewers. A short, simple questionnaire that is to be administered in all parts of the country would not justify the cost and effort of bringing all the interviewers together. A telephone briefing backed by notes or notes alone would, in these circumstances, be sufficient. Some market research agencies use tapes to deliver their briefing messages, although these are usually accompanied by a written summary.

The questionnaires can be given to the interviewers at the briefing. In the case of a telephone briefing, they can be sent directly to the interviewers (or to the area supervisor who distributes them). The questionnaires must be well packed to withstand a battering in the post. Padded postal bags are ideal.

Obtaining an interview

How to win public co-operation.

Some market researchers never carry out field interviews as they have interviewers who are trained for this purpose. However, the quality of all market research is dependent on asking the right questions of the right people and the interviewer plays a fundamental part in its equation. It is worth considering in some detail the role of the interviewer and the different approaches that can be adopted to win co-operation from the public. (Many of the principles are also appropriate in business-to-business surveys where the researcher is very often the interviewer.)

- *Be pleasant.* It seems trite, but it is a fact that a smile is more likely to win co-operation than a serious face or a frown. Even on the telephone, a smile is communicated by a more pleasant voice and a more pleasant voice will win co-operation.
- *Assure the respondent that the research is genuine.* Most interviews in this country are carried out by interviewers who are members of the interviewer card scheme operated by the Market Research Society. This is a scheme that requires the agency employing the interviewer, as well as the interviewer, to abide by certain standards. Each interviewer has an identity card with her name and photo. This is shown to respondents before the interview takes place so they can be assured that it really is a bona fide market research survey and not an attempt to sell something.
- *Come straight to the point.* It is far better to tell someone in plain language what you are doing than to use a long-winded explanation.
- *Explain what is required of the respondent.* If it will take 10 minutes to answer the questions, it is better to say so and avoid having to terminate the interview half-way through so that the respondent can catch a bus.
- *Be positive in approach and get straight into the questioning.* After the brief introduction, lose no time before asking the first question. A positive and assumptive approach will win co-operation and make the respondent feel the interview is professionally managed.

Explain what is required of the respondent.

Carrying out an interview

The first rule of carrying out a good interview is to *know the questionnaire* – inside out and backwards. Interviewers should spend time reading and re-reading the questionnaire so that they are totally familiar with the routing instructions, when to show cards, when to prompt and not to prompt, etc. It is no good assuming that these things can be learned during the first few interviews as they most certainly would be badly executed.

Know the questionnaire.

The interview should be looked upon as having a beginning, a middle and an end. Each of these parts of the interview needs careful and different treatment.

1. The beginning of the interview

At the start of the interview, respondents will be apprehensive. There will be tension from not knowing what they have let themselves in for.

- Some will have 'examination fears', believing that they may be asked questions to which they will not know the answers. They will fear being made to look stupid.
- Some will worry about the confidentiality of their responses. In business-to-business interviews, this can be a serious concern, while in domestic interviewing it can be a problem where personal or sensitive matters are discussed.
- Some respondents will try to assert their own status on the interviewer. This could manifest itself as arrogance or bossiness and the interviewer must avoid retaliating in kind.

It is in the first minutes of contact with the respondent that the interview is won or lost.

It is in the first minutes of contact with the respondent that the interview is won or lost. The interviewer must aim to do three things, and all of them quickly:

- Explain exactly what the survey is about in general terms. In this explanation, a quick exposé of the subjects is given and, if possible, the overall purpose of the work is disclosed.
- Tell the respondent what is required, again in broad terms. This could cover the length of time the interview is expected to take place and the type of questions that will be covered.
- Lead into the first question as quickly as possible, so that the respondent can begin to talk and gain confidence.

The first questions asked in the interview must be carefully chosen to take the tension out of the interview. They must, therefore, be easy to answer and not too controversial. Furthermore, they must have some relevance to the subject. In a business-to-business interview, it may be appropriate to have a lead-in question that asks: 'And how is business right now?' In an interview with a domestic consumer, a more focused question should lead into the questionnaire. For example, in a survey about milk, it would be appropriate to ask a simple question about how the milk is purchased: 'Can I start by asking if you have your milk delivered most days of the week?' Thereafter, questions can find out how often the milk is delivered, whether milk is bought from shops and how much is consumed per week.

2. The core of the interview

As the interview progresses, tension should begin to ease and the respondent will warm to the task of answering the questions. It is in the core of the interview that most time is spent. Now the interviewer has the problems of ensuring that accurate responses are obtained and interest is maintained. If the questioning goes on for more than half an hour, it is difficult to keep respondents interested, unless the subject is very dear to their hearts. Towards the back end of the interview, if a respondent is flagging, it could be appropriate to add a few words of encouragement.

Ensure that accurate responses are obtained.

In a structured interview, it is important that the interviewer sticks rigidly to the question as it has been designed. Quite clearly, problems will occur if 20 interviewers all put their own interpretation on how a question can be improved. Also, the interviewer must be careful not to lay emphasis on certain words in the question and so alter their meaning. Say to yourself the following question with the emphasis on the words in italics and you will see how the meaning changes subtly:

Stick rigidly to the question as it has been designed.

- '*How* do you like your steak cooked?'
- 'How do *you* like your steak cooked?'
- 'How do you like you *steak* cooked?'
- 'How do you like your steak *cooked*?'

As the interview is drawing to a close, the tension that existed at the beginning of the interview will largely have been removed and the respondents will be at their most relaxed. If questions of a sensitive nature are to be asked, it should be now. Classification questions can seem intrusive to respondents since the reason for asking them is not always clear. The time to ask them is, therefore, at the end.

Questions of a sensitive nature should be left to the end.

3. Concluding the interview

Throughout the interview, the interviewer must retain the initiative and bring it to a close firmly and professionally. If the interviewer does not acquire this skill, it is easy to get caught up in general conversation, from which it is difficult to extricate oneself.

The respondent must be thanked and given any final instructions, if these are relevant. In a product test, for example, there may be a follow-up interview at some time in the future; therefore, the respondent should

Ensure that any final instructions are given.

115

be told when this will be and precisely what should be done when, after testing the product.

The Market Research Society make small 'thank you' cards available to all companies that take part in their Card Carrying Scheme. It is good public relations for the market research industry to give these away. Moreover, the card gives the name and address of the market research company carrying out the study as a further reassurance that it is bona fide.

In an industrial interview, the respondent may have been promised a summary of the findings and he should be advised as to when these could be expected. At the very least, it would not be difficult to organise sending a letter of thanks.

4. Overcoming objections

Winning the co-operation of respondents is not always straightforward. Objections are sometimes raised and the interviewer must be ready to counter them. Of course, objections are sometimes entirely valid and must be respected. For example, in a business-to-business survey, it would be silly to interview someone who claimed to be the wrong person to speak to. The temptation to grab someone and persuade that person to take part, just because he is there, must be resisted.

Respect valid objections.

If a respondent is concerned about an issue, it may be possible to offer a short, satisfactory explanation. Certainly, the interviewer should not get into an argument that potentially could lead to complaints to the managers of the agency or the client. A number of commonly voiced objections and possible rejoinders are:

- Lack of time: 'The interview only lasts 10 minutes. I can call back at a more convenient time if you prefer, perhaps later this afternoon or tomorrow.'
- Lack of interest: The response to this objection requires *enthusiasm* on the part of the interviewer. It is not simply what is said but how it is said that matters. For example: 'It will only take a few minutes and I am sure that you will find it interesting.'
- Fear of not being able to answer the questions: 'The questions are quite straightforward. You don't have to know anything special; it's your opinion and views that count.'
- Worry over confidentiality: 'The interview is being done to a strict

code of ethics and you can be assured that every response is pooled so that no single reply can be linked to a person.'
- Dislike of intrusion or general suspicion: 'I understand, as I feel the same. However, surveys are important because they enable us to find out about products and services so that improvements can be made.' Alternatively: 'I can promise you that this is a bona fide survey. Your replies will be treated in strict confidence and no one will try to sell you anything as a result of helping me.'

5. Personal issues

Interviewers should look smart, since they are representing not just themselves but their companies and all their colleagues who may have to follow in their footsteps. Usually, the interviewer does not have the chance to make a great personal impact on a respondent, since they will only be in contact for just a short period. In these circumstances, the interviewer may not be able to rely on features of personality and competence, which take some time to shine through.

The interviewer's appearance and manner are important.

As with appearance, other personal matters are very much common sense. A warm smile can be a strong weapon in winning the co-operation of respondents, and a positive and confident manner will help the respondent to feel more at ease. A clipboard and questionnaire at the ready and a poised pen look business-like.

Equally, there are some things that should be avoided. It is not good policy for interviewers to call on respondents smelling of alcohol. Spicy foods should be given a miss if the interviewer is going to stand a couple of feet away, asking questions and breathing over the respondent.

Types of interview

1. Street interviews

Street interviews is a term that market researchers use to cover all types of interviewing carried out in public places. Often, they are carried out in busy streets in the centre of urban areas but equally they could be carried out in shopping precincts, at railway stations or motorway service stations (where permission from the operator is required). Street interviews are one of the most popular methods of data collection in consumer market research. They are relatively inexpensive to under-take as it is possible for an interviewer to achieve between 20 and 40 per day depending on any quota restrictions. (This is three to four times the number that can be achieved in the home.)

Street interviews are usually carried out while the respondent and the interviewer are standing up. Respondents are asked to co-operate while going about their daily business, so it is to be expected that most people will have only limited time available to help in a survey. The questionnaire should not take more than 10 minutes, although 5 minutes is preferable. As this does not allow much time for probing, street interviews are not the occasion to undertake depth work. They are most suitable for checking out simple questions; those that can be answered quickly and which do not require too much thought on the part of the respondent.

Street interviews should be kept as simple as possible.

Street interviews are hard work for the interviewer who is standing all day, often in cold, draughty or wet conditions. It is not the ideal environment for writing lengthy verbatim replies to questions. Ideally, street interview questionnaires should consist mainly of pre-coded responses with boxes to tick or numbers to circle.

When organising street interviews, the following points should be remembered:

- Provide sufficient questionnaires and prompt cards for the job.
- Explain what quota instructions must be met.
- State where interviews can and cannot take place.
- State how many interviews must be carried out at an interviewing point.
- Give a telephone number where the interviewer can get hold of someone who is controlling the survey, if help or guidance is needed.
- Give clear instructions of what should be returned when the work is finished. (For example, in addition to the questionnaires, it may be important to return any prompt cards, quota sheets, etc.).
- Seek written permission from any organisations on whose property the interviewing will take place (shopping centres, service stations, etc.).
- Advise any officials that the survey is being carried out, should this be relevant. (Some surveys can engender suspicion among respondents and it may be a precaution to advise the police that a survey is being carried out. This would avoid any problems if a member of the public reports the interviewer to the police as a suspicious person.)

2. Interviews in the home

Interviewing in the home is carried out when:

- The interview is lengthy (the interviewer and the respondent are under cover, and can sit down if necessary)
- Reference may need to be made to something in the home (for example, the brand and model of a product may need to be established)
- The research method may require home interviews (for example, with preselected addresses or in a random sample where every '*n*th' house is chosen)

Additional points to be remembered when interviewing in the home are:

- Interviewing should be carried out at *reasonable* times of the day. Market research is a vital and necessary means of finding out what people do and how they think, but it is intrusive and it is important that researchers are considerate towards the people from whom they collect information. For example, it can be disturbing to have interviewers knock on the door after 8.30 in the evening and at any time on Sunday.
- Up to three calls should be made on a home if, on the first two occasions, the respondent is not in. When addresses are preselected or form part of a random interviewing programme, the interviewer should be instructed to keep returning, at different times of day and on different days, to try to get hold of the respondent. Otherwise, the survey would be biased by excluding busy people, those who work and those who have lots of interests outside the home.

Interviewing in the home should be carried out at reasonable times of the day.

3. Telephone interviews

Telephone interviews have gained in popularity as a market research tool over the last decade as over 80 per cent of households and all businesses are accessible by this means. Sat at the telephone with a list of contacts and telephone numbers, an interviewer can get through four 10-minute interviews per hour – and these can be preselected addresses or a random sample of households anywhere in the country. The cost of interviewing over the telephone may not be any less than a street interview, but the ability to select households and obtain random samples means that the sampling quality may be better (although it has to be remembered that one-fifth of all households are not on the telephone, and a further fifth are ex-directory, which introduces some bias into telephone samples).

The telephone is not a means of randomly sampling people, since the researcher does not know the composition of the family unit selected. If the interview, in every case, is with the housewife, then ignorance of the composition of the make-up of the family is no disadvantage. However, if a true random sample of people is required, some form of rotational grid must be devised to give all members of the household a chance of selection.

The conventions of when to call on homes and how often to call are equally applicable to telephone surveys.

Some points to remember when carrying out telephone interviews are:

- It is vital that the interviewer ascertains who is on the other end of the telephone. For example, the interview may be required with the male head of the household and confusion could easily occur if the telephone was answered by a teenage son with a mature voice.
- Since the interviewer cannot see the respondent, it is not possible to observe facial reactions to questions which, in face-to-face interviews, can lead to probing or qualifying notes. Nor does the interviewer know if anyone else is in earshot of the respondent and the extent to which this is affecting the answers. For these reasons, it may be important to check at the outset if it is convenient to talk.
- There are obvious limitations to the types of question that can be asked over the telephone. It is not possible to use display material of any kind – prompt cards, adverts, products, etc.
- It is harder to keep a respondent's interest on the telephone than it is when face to face. This means that a telephone interview has to be short. Ten minutes is a reasonable guideline as a maximum for the telephone, but it can be longer if the subject is really engaging. (However, because less chit-chat takes place over the telephone, it is a highly productive medium and 10 minutes could be equivalent to 15 minutes face to face.)

Business telephone interviews. Telephone interviews carried out with respondents in business are very similar in principle to those in the home. Of course, the time at which business respondents can be contacted is limited to business hours, whereas telephone interviews with householders are often carried out in

120

the early evening. Also the business respondent is more conditioned to answering questions over the telephone, although there may be hurdles to straddle before contact is made.

In a business-to-business interview, the interviewer may only know the *position* of the respondent and not the person's name. This means that the co-operation of the receptionist and, perhaps, a secretary must be enlisted before being put through to the right person. Even then, the availability of the person concerned may be limited by meetings or pressures of work. And once the interviewer has been put through, it cannot be assumed that the respondent will have an answer for everything, nor necessarily be in a position to answer all the questions. Purchasing decisions in business involve a number of people and the person who specifies which product to buy may not know its price or anything about a company's sales service. A respondent in a business-to-business interview may not feel able to give away the size and strength of his company to an unseen and unknown person on the other end of a telephone. In these circumstances, some subtlety is clearly required in the asking of the questions. For example, the question 'Which company do you buy from?' may appear too blunt when asked over the telephone. Since supplier information is usually regarded as sensitive, it may be better to ease the respondent into the subject. For example, it would be better to ask the following three questions which lead naturally from one to the other:

- 'Which of the suppliers of product x do you know?'
- 'Which of these companies do you think is best overall?'
- 'And which of these companies have you ever used?'

Carrying out postal surveys

Postal surveys are not frequently used in market research because the response rates are hard to predict, they are hard to control and one can never be sure if those who have replied are representative of those who have not. Response rates vary enormously and depend on the subject, the length of the questionnaire, the types of question asked, plus a host of other minor factors. British Gas has an authority attached to its name which helps it to achieve response rates of over 50 per cent from postal surveys, while in many industrial subjects the researcher is lucky to get more than 10 per cent returned. Nevertheless, postal surveys have an appeal if you are working with few resources and no staff. One person can mail out hundreds or thousands of questionnaires and sit back to await the response. There is no need to book interviewers or to arrange briefing sessions, and there are no problems of getting the interviewers' work back in and checked.

1. Factors affecting the response rates in postal questionnaires

The interest factor

Use postal surveys when respondents are likely to be highly motivated to reply.

The main factor influencing the response rate of a postal survey is the interest that respondents have in the subject. People are far more likely to respond to a questionnaire asking them about the new car they have just bought than one that asks about their buying habits of toothpaste. Thus, researchers should avoid using postal surveys except when respondents are likely to be highly motivated to reply.

The incentive
Respondents do not want to feel that their efforts in completing the questionnaire are a waste of time. It is important, therefore, that a powerful cover letter is written that explains the purpose of the study and convinces the recipients that their replies matter. If possible, respondents should be given some benefit. This could be the intangible promise of better products or service, or a tangible gift.

The layout
The questionnaire must be orderly, logical and look appealing. Ideally, it should be typeset (or desk-top published) and litho printed. A professionally produced questionnaire will lift the response.

The convenience factor
The successful self-completion questionnaire must be easy to complete, requiring the respondent simply to tick boxes wherever possible. The enclosure of a stamped addressed envelope (or at least a business reply envelope) will raise the response in consumer surveys, although less so in industrial surveys, where respondents have envelopes and franking machines to hand.

2. Designing cover letters for postal questionnaires

The cover letter that accompanies the questionnaire is as important as the questionnaire itself. Unless there is absolute certainty about the name and position of the respondent, it is better to address the letter using a general title, such as 'Dear Householder'. In a business-to-business survey, it may be addressed to a person responsible for a function, such as 'The Buyer' or 'The Works Manager'.

Rules that should be applied to the writing of a good cover letter are:

- Explain what the survey is about and why the respondent has been selected.
- As with telephone interviewing, give the respondent a reason for wanting to complete the questionnaire – offer a benefit of one kind or another.
- Give clear instructions about what to do – how to fill in the questionnaire, how to send it back, etc.
- Give an assurance that completing the questionnaire is easy.
- If it is possible to do so, give an assurance that replies will be confidential.
- Thank the respondent.

Overleaf is an example of a typical cover letter:

3. Checklist for organising the postal survey
Many components and tasks are involved in a postal survey and the researcher should follow a checklist to ensure that each is carried out successfully.

At the beginning

- Decide what day you are going to mail. (Try to 'land' it on a Tuesday or Wednesday – the week's mail that has not been actioned by Friday stands a good chance of being 'binned'. Avoid holiday periods.)
- Decide how many people you are going to mail.
- Decide whether you are going to address the people personally or generically (for example, Dear Householder).
- Decide if you are going to offer a tangible incentive.

Organising the production of the questionnaire

- Draft the questionnaire and check it out on a few people before finalising. Keep the length to four sides of A4.
- Send the questionnaire to the printers together with instructions on layout, printing deadline and the number of questionnaires required.

Business & Market Research plc

MARKETING CONSULTANTS

BUXTON ROAD, HIGH LANE, STOCKPORT, CHESHIRE SK6 8DX
Telephone (0663) 65115   Fax (0663) 62362

John Smith Esq
Works Director
Electronic Assembly Ltd
The Science Park
Cambridge CR4 5ZW

Dear Mr Smith

I am carrying out a project to find out the attitudes of buyers and specifiers to suppliers of printed circuit boards. The aims of the study are wide ranging but it is especially important that I obtain the views of a cross section of users of boards. I am, therefore, writing to a number of carefully selected people, across the country, to ask for their help. I believe that you are a user of printed circuit boards and I would appreciate just a few minutes of your time to answer the questions in the enclosed questionnaire.

Your reply is very important to me. I should also emphasise that it is an opportunity for you to express your views which hopefully will lead to improved products and services.

Be assured that your reply will be treated as absolutely confidential. The responses will be pooled and no individual replies will be singled out or traced back.

All you have to do is to read through the questions and tick the boxes which best describe your answers. Please remember that there is no one correct answer; it is your opinion that counts. When you have finished, return the questionnaire in the enclosed stamped addressed envelope. I am working to a tight timetable so I would appreciate it greatly if you could get it in the post as soon as possible.

May I thank you in advance for your co-operation and I look forward to receiving your reply.

Yours sincerely

Paul Hague
Director
January 1, 1990

BUSINESS
& MARKET
RESEARCH PLC

Registered Office as above   Registered No. 1158270 (England)

124

(Arrange to have 10 per cent more printed than will be needed as 'spares' are always useful.)
- Consider having the questionnaire printed on different coloured paper to help to identify the responses from different groups of people.
- Check the proof of the questionnaire before the printing run takes place.

Organising the reply envelope

- Check what size of envelope is required for the replies – it should be able to take the questionnaire folded in half. Order the number of envelopes for the survey plus 10 per cent for spares.
- Check that you have a current business reply number; if not, arrange for one at the local post office (or decide to use stamps).
- Find a printer who can print your company name and the business reply decal on the envelope (not all printers can print on envelopes). Give the printer instructions.

Organising the cover letter

- Write the cover letter and 'polish' it until it has the correct impact.
- Arrange for the printing of the cover letter and, if you cannot bear the thought of signing hundreds of letters, arrange for the signature to be reproduced in blue.

Organising the lists of respondents

- Decide on the source of respondents and arrange to obtain a copy. Make sure that you specify how you want the list – on labels, on disk, with named respondents (or not), etc.
- Check the list for any unwanted data. Get it on to a database or word-processing system, if necessary.
- Print out the labels or the names and addresses on to the letterheads. Have a spare list printed for control purposes.

Organising the incentive

- Make sure that the incentive is suitable for mailing in the post.
- Order a sufficient number of incentives and make sure that they will be delivered with a few days' grace prior to the mailing.

Organising stuffing the envelopes

- If you need to know the names of companies or people who subsequently respond, mark the questionnaires and attribute numbers to them on the sampling list.
- Arrange help for stuffing the envelopes.
- Give the post room some notice or, if necessary, take the packed envelopes to the local sorting office.

As the replies come in

- Count the replies in daily so you can see when the response is falling off. Decide when to cut off the response and run the analysis (usually within two to three weeks).
- If you are checking which individuals have responded, note their codes on the returned questionnaires and check them against the same code on the list of respondents mailed.
- Code the questionnaires ready for analysis.

◀ CHAPTER 6 ▶

OTHER RESEARCH TECHNIQUES

In this chapter, we look at the use of group discussions and hall tests. Although both techniques involve bringing respondents to the place where the fieldwork is carried out, these two methods differ in other respects.

Groups are a *qualitative* research method involving small samples. Various material may be shown to respondents attending groups but this is not the essence of the approach.

Hall tests are a *quantitative* technique, involving significant-sized samples, and they are held so that respondents can see, handle or taste things that cannot be practically shown in the street or home.

Group discussions

A group is a meeting of respondents – typically eight, but possibly ranging from four to fifteen – who meet and discuss a subject. A researcher – the group leader or moderator – guides and leads the meeting. The aim of the meeting is to generate a *discussion* among the respondents rather than to seek responses to a series of formal questions. For a particular project, a number of such groups are organised. Four, six or eight groups are common, but more, or sometimes less, may be used. The proceedings of a group are audio or even video recorded so that they can be analysed at a later date.

Group discussions should be used to obtain qualitative data.

The group technique is equally applicable in consumer and business-to-business research. When selecting it as an appropriate technique, however, it is important to bear in mind that it should be used to obtain qualitative rather than quantitative data. In Chapter 1, the difference between qualitative and quantitative research was defined. Rather than counting and measuring, qualitative research is concerned with understanding motivations and attitudes; the 'whys' rather than the 'how manys'. In a group discussion, questions may be asked to establish behaviour or preferences for one thing or another, but covering such areas is only a *means* to probing *why* the behaviour is carried out, or *why* one product or brand is preferred over another. Groups, for example, can be used to establish why a private pension scheme might be considered, or why one company's product might be preferred to another. If, however, we want to measure the proportion of the population that has a private pension, or the awareness level of one company compared to another, we should use quite different (quantitative) techniques.

Group discussions also offer the opportunity to give respondents information or show them things. We can, for example, show TV adverts for pensions. We might use concept sheets to give respondents some information in an easily digested form – for example, how the system for contracting out of the state pension scheme works – or show physical products and have respondents handle or taste them. However, groups should not be used for these reasons alone. If the data sought, in conjunction with showing material or products, is qualitative, then groups may be the best approach, but if we are seeking quantitative measures, then we should be using other techniques which allow exposure to the stimulus material – perhaps a hall test or home placement.

We will discuss the way in which group discussions should be carried out under four headings:

- Planning groups
- Group recruitment
- Leading groups
- Analysing groups

An important general point to bear in mind is that the time spent running the group – one or two hours – represents a small percentage of the effort that goes into using this technique. The time spent planning, recruiting and analysing the proceedings is far greater. Furthermore, a group may be well or badly led, but whatever the level of skill of the researcher leading it, something will come out of the work. This, however, pre-supposes that planning and recruitment have resulted in a group meeting at all; if this part of the work is skimped or ill managed, the respondents making up the group may just not arrive.

1. Planning groups
Planning groups includes deciding:

- Who should be recruited
- The make-up of the sample and number of groups
- What is to be covered in the groups
- The appropriate venue
- What other physical resources are needed

(Recruitment must also be planned, but since this is an important issue, it will be discussed separately later.)

Who should be recruited
The first step in planning a group is deciding who the respondents are to be. In general terms, they must be *relevant* to the research objectives and such relevance may be in terms of any or several of the following criteria:

Decide who the respondents are to be.

- Demographics
- Status
- Behaviour
- Attitudes

Often, the composition of the group is defined in demographic terms. We, for example, aim to establish the attitudes surrounding private pensions and we may, therefore, recruit respondents who are likely to be able to afford private pension provision and are in the age groups targeted for selling pensions. We will certainly cover both men and women, unless for some reason we specifically wish to home-in on one sex.

Status or responsibility is the most common criterion used to select respondents in business-to-business groups. In this case, we aim to recruit respondents having a particular job title or responsibility for a particular decision – transport managers responsible for selecting the make of truck operated, architects involved in designing medium-sized commercial buildings, etc.

Recruitment by behaviour involves selecting those who carry out a specific task or function – for example, those who have taken out a private pension, those who regularly buy premium lager, financial managers who use a specific type of accounts software, and so on.

We may wish to hold a group of respondents with particular attitudes. Attitudes to a new food, among those with positive attitudes to 'health' foods or the environment, is one example.

Having set the respondent criteria, you should ensure that these are met by including relevant questions in the recruitment questionnaire.

The make-up of the sample
Closely linked to the setting of criteria for recruiting respondents is the process of deciding the number of groups to carry out, the numbers of people in each group and, therefore, the sample size. Group discussions are a qualitative technique and our aim is not to cover a sample large enough to be statistically significant. Other things being equal, a sample of 25 relevant respondents may be enough. Typically, groups consist of eight respondents and, therefore, a sample of 24 could be obtained from three groups. However, this assumes that we are covering a sample of only one homogenous population. This is seldom the case. We may, for example, wish to compare the attitudes of men and women; therefore, we need an acceptable sample size of both – perhaps 20 of each sex – increasing the total sample size to 40. Similarly, we may wish to represent adequate numbers from, say, two age groups and two social classes. A specimen planning matrix for a total sample of 64, by sex, age and social class, is:

	Males		**Females**	
	Over 35	Under 35	Over 35	Under 35
Class AB	8	8	8	8
Class C1C2	8	8	8	8

This gives 32 respondents in each category of three demographic criteria (each sex and age group is split into two categories – AB and C1C2). In analysis, we can, therefore, compare men and women, older and younger, and higher and lower status groups, and have equal sized subsamples in each case.

With eight respondents per group, the plan could be amended to show one group per cell (substituting one group per eight respondents). With this plan, therefore, we would end up with *homogenous* groups – one group of AB males under 35, one of AB males over 35, etc. Generally, it is better to aim for relatively homogenous groups; interaction and candour tend to be higher among equals. The need for homogeneity may, therefore, lead to larger samples, quite apart from a need to include adequate numbers of specific groupings. In the foregoing example, we may believe that class is not a particularly relevant factor and that there is no need to aim for 32 or so of the two classes. However, because we aim to hold homogenous groups, we still end up with four groups for each class and a total sample of 64.

Homogenous groups, while common, are not sacrosanct. We may deliberately wish to have an interaction between different types of respondent; a mix in terms of demographics or other variables and especially behaviour. In the plan given earlier, we could, for example, include equal numbers of users and non-users of a certain product in each group.

Our example has assumed that each group will consist of eight respondents, and this has implications for the number of groups required. If, in the example, we decide we need to cover two regions, take into account the other demographics and aim for homogenous groups, then 16 groups of eight would be required (try writing out the plan assuming two regions have to be covered). Eight is not magical, however, and the numbers in each group could be adjusted between, say, six and ten, purely to fit the sampling plan. Also, to some extent, the numbers per group are decided on the basis of the group leader's personal preference and style; some researchers are happier with six rather than ten, and vice versa. Beyond ten, groups generally become too large to run well, but even this is not an inviolable rule.

As in all research plans, budgets and timetables have to be considered when planning groups. Obviously, the more groups that are held, the higher the costs, and unless the number of group leaders is increased, the timetable will also need extending. Also, the time needed to analyse the results and write reports increases, perhaps more than in proportion to the number of groups. For such reasons, you may have to compromise and carry out fewer groups, but at least recognise where you are making compromises. We may, for example, reduce our numbers of groups from eight to four and, as a result, be less able to comment on differences in attitude between, say, under and over 35s. We may also have to settle for less homogenous groups than we would like and include some from both social classes in each group.

What is to be covered

Prepare a discussion guide.

Groups are meant to be flexible in the sense that the respondents are encouraged to develop ideas and discuss or argue each other's views, with the group leader's involvement continually tuned to the direction of the discussion. Before the groups are held, however, a topic checklist or discussion guide should be prepared. This should cover: how the subject and purpose of the research is to be introduced at the group, the topics that should be covered as a minimum, the order in which they are to be covered (if this is important), and when and what to show if respondent information or another stimulus is to be used in the research.

It is important to think about how the subject of the research and the nature of the discussion is to be introduced. Often, respondents are uncertain about why they are attending a group and so they will need reassurance on this before they will feel able to contribute. They also need to understand what they are expected to do (for example, talk while the group leader listens). A group leader will normally develop a personal style for starting the group and this aspect of the introduction does not need covering in the topic checklist. What specifically is to be discussed is, however, unique to each series of groups and should be defined in the checklist. It may be desirable to confine the description of the discussion topics to a very general level and then become more specific as the discussion develops; this needs careful thought and should be covered in the checklist.

Unlike a structured questionnaire, the precise wording used in a checklist is seldom critical; it may well be changed during or between groups. The group leader, however, must be certain about what is to be covered and, therefore, the checklist must be clear and unambiguous. Often, the sequence of topics is loose and may be changed to fit how the discussion develops – something towards the end of the checklist may be raised by a respondent early on and discussed there and then. There may, however, be some sequences that need to be adhered to and these must be clearly indicated in the checklist. General attitudes about a product, for example, are logically discussed before the group is asked to think about specific brands.

The checklist will also describe how and when stimulus material is to be used. Again, it may be desirable to introduce it only after certain topics have been discussed.

Successful groups never have enough time, so it may be useful to indicate on the checklist how much time should be allocated to each major subject. However, this is strictly for guidance only and should not be regarded as a rigid timetable. Similarly, some topics may be considered more vital than others (key topics) while others may be introduced only as a means of encouraging discussion in important areas (procedural rather than substantive topics) – we may ask a group of, say, maintenance managers to describe their routine jobs, to help them think about the problems they face in their work. It can be useful to distinguish, by the use of different typestyles, underlining or bolding, such key, substantive and procedural topics.

As an example, part of a group topic checklist is shown in Figure 6.1.

Where appropriate, any prompt material will have to be prepared. This can include:

Prepare any prompt material.

- *Concept boards.* These can include written statements – be brief and use simple words, sketches and diagrams, paste-ups of illustrations and actual or mock adverts. The size and lettering have to be adequate, bearing in mind the size of the room to be used.
- *Videos.* Obviously, these will be prepared for the researcher. Remember the appropriate equipment will be needed.
- *Products.* Think carefully about how these are to be shown – for example, with brands hidden or visible? Also, how are they to be concealed from respondents if it is planned to show them after some preliminary discussion?
- *Self-completion material.* This might include plain paper and pencils for writing or sketching, modelling clay and self-completion questionnaires. Their role is discussed when we consider how to run a group.

Introduction
- Introduction of respondents (to each other).
- Introduction of moderator and research company.
- Explain purpose of discussion and reason for tapes.
- Introduce subject and material to be used.

Warm up
- Attitudes towards local rail travel (getting all moans out of the way if necessary). If necessary, comparing local travel with inter-city travel to ensure focus on the former.
- Advantages (and disadvantages) of local rail journeys over other methods such as car and bus.

Leisure only
- Places people currently go on leisure trips (any places they want to visit but, for whatever reason, can't). When they go and how they get there. Where do they think they could go for days out by train?

Commuters only
- Where do they think they can commute to?
- How long do they think it would take them to get to work on the train?
- Perceptions of travelling to work on the train.
- Awareness of any recent changes to local trains (new direct destinations from their station?).
- New trains (sprinters in Hazel Grove?).
- Explanation of flipchart and recording – imagine it's a finished TV ad.

ROTATE ORDER OF ADS

Leisure travellers only
Mother and son on day out – **SHOW ONCE**

- Immediate (spontaneous) impact/impression: What is the ad saying? Can they identify with it?
- Then explanation of ad in more detail.
- Now what do they think? Likes and dislikes? Relevance (with them and with their expectation of the local railway network)?
- How could it be improved? Persuasiveness?
- Attitudes towards characters and storyline?
- Understanding of:
    Windsor link
    Ad is saying how things have changed
    More direct routes fewer changes
    Trains are now more frequent and on time

Figure 6.1 *Specimen discussion guide*

The appropriate venue

Venue choice includes deciding on the type of rooms in which to hold the groups, their location and timing.

Consumer groups are generally held in private houses: often the home of the interviewer carrying out the recruitment, and, in practice, you tend to accept the room made available. However, the ideal room satisfies the following requirements:

- Large enough to hold the anticipated number of respondents plus any material to be shown and equipment (e.g. video), without crowding
- Have adequate seating, preferably all equally comfortable
- Be heated to an acceptable temperature but with adequate ventilation
- Have adequate furniture for any refreshments – respondents should not have to clutch their cups all evening
- Plain, simple and non-distracting decor
- Away from intrusive noise

For most purposes, a room of this sort is adequate, but if video recording is to be used or if the group is to be observed over closed-circuit television, a hotel room might be used even for consumer groups. Alternatively, a few purpose-built facilities can be rented.

For business-to-business groups, it is more usual to hire a hotel room than use a private house. Unfortunately, this often creates additional problems; for example, the hotel management often do not understand what is required and do not supply the facilities at all or bring them at the wrong time. The following checklist may help:

Choice of hotel
- Is it easy to find?
- Is parking adequate if respondents are expected to travel by car?
- Is the status of the hotel commensurate with respondents?

Choice of room
- Is the size right for the number of respondents and equipment required?
- Will noise levels be acceptable?

- Is the access adequate, bearing in mind any material or equipment that has to be accommodated?

Letting the hotel know your requirements
- Specify in advance the times the room is needed, including preparation and clearing up time.
- The seating plan required, e.g. board table or informal.

It is always best to inspect a hotel venue before it is booked. This particularly applies to the size and siting of rooms; never rely on the hotel's own claims. If you cannot visit the hotel, at least ask for a floor plan with dimensions. Let the hotel know, in writing, of your requirements and allow enough time before the group starts to sort out problems.

The location of the venue has to suit the convenience of the respondents invited.

The location of the venue, whether a private home or hotel, has to suit the convenience of the respondents invited. Groups involving respondents with children at private schools will be held at a home in or near a middle class suburb. City centre office workers are best invited to a central and well-known hotel. A business-to-business group with respondents drawn from a 20-mile radius might be most likely to come to a venue just off a motorway junction.

Groups, whether consumer or business to business, are usually held in the early to middle evening – starting at 6.30 or 7 pm. Sometimes lunchtime can be considered for shorter business-to-business groups and afternoons for consumer respondents who are not working.

The duration of a group can range from under an hour to several hours. One to one-and-a-half hours is typical and usually adequate for most subjects. Anything under one hour seems a waste of the recruitment effort. Groups with durations of over one-and-a-half hours are harder to recruit and can be more expensive, since it is not possible to squeeze two into an evening.

Other physical resources
A checklist of equipment and material to take to a group is essential:

- Name and address of venue
- Date and time the groups are arranged

- Names of interviewers involved in recruitment or hosting the group
- Topic checklists
- Prompt materials
- Equipment needed
- Paper or any questionnaires needed by respondents
- Pens or pencils
- Tape recorder(s)
- Tapes
- Spare batteries or mains extension leads
- Stands needed for any equipment
- Incentives (money or gift)

Always assume the worst with tape recorders and take two – better still, use two together. Similarly, have spare tapes with you. Above all, know how to work the equipment; failures are often due to ignorance.

Although audio recording is the normal practice, video recording can be used as well and occasionally the proceedings may be shown live to observers, over closed-circuit television. One-way mirrors are also sometimes used for this purpose. However, these are all expensive complications and you need to have good reasons for using them.

2. Group recruitment

As already mentioned, recruitment is a vital part of group work. Unless this is successful, the group will be a failure.

Unless recruitment is successful, the group will be a failure.

The general principles of recruitment apply to both consumer and business-to-business groups, but there are quite substantial differences in detail, so each is considered separately.

Consumer groups
Consumer group recruitment is normally carried out by an interviewer and very often it is the interviewer's home that is used as the venue. A group recruitment sheet, as shown in Figure 6.2, is used to tell the interviewer who should be recruited for each group. A recruitment questionnaire is also usually used. This both provides a record of who attends the group and guides the interviewer in establishing whether a respondent meets the recruitment criteria. A specimen questionnaire is given in Figure 6.3.

Project no: 13389   **Group no:**   A

Date of group: 12 September 1990

Starting time: 7 pm   **Expected finishing time:**   8.15 pm

Venue: 12 Orchard Avenue, Oldham, Greater Manchester

Recruiter: Jessie Richards   **Telephone no:**   0663 65115

Incentive: £8.50

Total no of respondents:		<u>8</u>
Sex:	Female	<u>8</u>
Social class:	BC1	<u>8</u>
Age:	35/45	<u>8</u>
Pension arrangement: In company scheme		4
In private scheme		<u>4</u>
		8

Notes: See recruitment questionnaire for definitions of pension arrangements

Figure 6.2 *Group recruitment sheet*

The interviewer's job is twofold:

- Locate respondents who meet the recruitment criteria
- Persuade them to attend the group

Generally, respondents are recruited from within a fairly small catchment area; a few miles from the venue and involving only up to 15 minutes' travel from home. Potential respondents are approached in shopping areas or by calling at their homes. Where the recruitment criterion is particularly difficult (for example, caravan owners who have taken their vans abroad in the last two years), various forms of referral may have to be used – one respondent can suggest someone else who may qualify. On initial approach, the interviewer can go through the recruitment questionnaire with the respondent without mentioning attendance at a group; in this way, the effort of persuasion is required only for relevant respondents.

Good morning/afternoon/evening I'm _____ (SHOW IDENTITY CARD) from B&MR Consumer, an independent market research company. We are carrying out a survey on tinned meats. Could you spare a few minutes of your time to answer some questions?

We are looking for people who work in certain occupations. Do you or anyone else in your household work in any of the following occupations? (SHOW SCREENER.)

- Advertising   1
- Journalism   2
- Marketing   3   CLOSE
- Market research   4
- Food manufacturing   5
- Food retailing   6
- None of these   7   CONTINUE

Q1 First, do you use either tinned ham, chopped ham and pork or luncheon meat nowadays?

- Tinned ham   1
- Chopped ham and pork   2
- Luncheon meat   3
- None   4   CLOSE

Q2 And which make of these products do you usually purchase? (READ OUT.)

- Celebrity   1
- Princes   2
- Plumrose   3
- Ye Olde Oak   4
- Dak   5
- Any others   X
  _____
- None   Y

IF CELEBRITY PURCHASED, RECRUIT TO GROUP AS USER QUOTA AND ASK Q4

IF DOES NOT PURCHASE CELEBRITY, GO TO Q3

Q3 (ASK THOSE NOT PURCHASING CELEBRITY.) Thinking again about the different manufacturers of tinned ham, chopped ham and pork and luncheon meat, have you heard of any of the following. (READ OUT.)

- Princes   1
- Plumrose   2
- Celebrity   3   RECRUIT
- Ye Olde Oak   4
- Dak   5

IF AWARE OF CELEBRITY, RESPONDENT IS ELIGIBLE

CHECK CLASSIFICATION DETAILS AND RECRUIT TO QUOTA

Q4 (ASK ALL.) Have you attended a market research group discussion in the last six months?

- Yes   1   DO NOT RECRUIT
- No   2   RECRUIT

GIVE DETAILS OF GROUP LOCATION AND TIME

I hereby declare that I have carried this interview out according to your instructions with the person named above

Interviewer's name _____

Interviewer's signature _____

Date _____

Figure 6.3 *Specimen recruitment questionnaire*

Persuasion involves describing what the respondent is being asked to do (that is, attend a group discussion) and 'selling' the benefits of attendance:

- You will find it an interesting and enjoyable meeting.
- You will be helping companies to offer better products.
- There will be some wine/coffee/snacks, etc.
- You will receive a gift in appreciation of your help.

The gift is only a small token of thanks and so a gift of fairly modest value is adequate. Generally, cash is easiest to organise (the recruiter can be given an advance to make the cash available) and almost all respondents find this form of incentive acceptable.

Sell the benefits of attendance.

Respondents will need to feel that attending the group will not involve some hidden catch:

- We are not selling anything. This is just market research and you will not be asked to buy anything.
- And there will not be any follow-up. Nobody will be asking you to do anything else afterwards.
- We just want to hear your opinions. You don't need to have any special knowledge about anything.
- All you will be asked to do is chat. Nothing else.

The result sought from the recruitment is eight (or however many) relevant, consenting respondents, who can be confidently expected to turn up on the night. With this in mind, a firm promise should be sought. It is better to discourage lukewarm respondents than be uncertain of the eventual turn-out. For this reason, the group should not be over-sold.

Get a firm commitment from the respondent.

The recruiter should follow up and reinforce the respondent's commitment with a written invitation and, ideally, by calling at the respondent's home – delivering the written invitation can be the excuse for a visit. Telephone reminders can be used as well, with perhaps a final call an hour or so before the group is due to start. Allowing for such follow-up, the recruitment can span several days:

Follow up and reinforce the respondent's commitment.

- Day 1 – Screening and recruitment of respondents
- Day 3 – Written invitation delivered to respondent's home
- Day 5 – Group meeting preceded by reminder telephone call

Even with the follow-up and reinforcement, it is best to be pessimistic and have 'cross-my-heart' promises from more than the number of respondents required – perhaps ten for the eight sought. If all the extras do turn up, it is usually possible to include them in the group; two too many is better than two too few.

Business-to-business groups
The principles of recruiting business-to-business groups are the same as

those for consumer groups but with some important differences in detailed approach. A group of this type normally consists of respondents who have a specific type of responsibility or job title in their work – for example, architects, electricians, stationery buyers, transport managers, etc. – and are perhaps drawn from a particular industry. Clearly, screening to locate relevant respondents has to involve contact at the place of work and the telephone is the best tool to use.

A screening questionnaire and recruitment sheet of basically the same type as for consumer are groups used, but in this case the recruiting interviewers work on the telephone. An initial contact sample is drawn up and written out on interviewers' contact sheets. This includes organisations that are likely to yield relevant respondents. If architect groups are to be recruited, the list could be drawn from a relevant professional directory. If groups of transport managers are needed, the contact sample could be a list of any manufacturing or distribution companies.

As well as the industry or activity of the organisation, included in the initial contact list, location is also important. While it is possible to persuade respondents to travel long distances to attend a group, the problems and uncertainties of recruitment increase with the size of the catchment area. Wherever possible, it is better to recruit respondents who only need to come a few miles to the group venue – half an hour's journey at the most.

Business-to-business respondents are also offered incentives, the value of which may be a little higher than is typical in consumer research. However, it is important to understand that the incentive is really a token of thanks and increasing the value will not significantly affect the success of the recruitment. Many respondents incur travel costs (these are not usually reimbursed) which are nearly as much as the incentive is worth. A bottle of whisky each is a common incentive at groups and offering two bottles apiece will make very little difference.

In the initial contact, the twin aims, as in consumer groups, are to establish whether the respondent is qualified – meets the criteria for inclusion – and to persuade the respondent to attend. The approach, in terms of the benefits to be suggested and overcoming objections, is exactly the same. Respondents, however, are more likely to say yes and mean no. Agreeing to a telephone request is an easy way of ending what

Business & Market Research plc

MARKETING CONSULTANTS

BUXTON ROAD, HIGH LANE, STOCKPORT, CHESHIRE SK6 8DX
Telephone (0663) 65115   Fax (0663) 62362

Dear

Thank you for agreeing to take part in our discussion group.

Please find enclosed your invitation to join us at The Crest Hotel, Welwyn Garden City, where we hope the hour you spend with us you will find both interesting and beneficial.

As a small thank you there will be a bottle of whisky for you to take home, together with some interesting products for you to test.

Please note, there are ample car parking facilities at the hotel and light refreshments will be served.

Yours sincerely

Shelagh Stokes
October 10, 1989

---

invitation

we shall be pleased to see you at our
Market Research Group Discussion

on _____ at _____

the meeting will be held at

_____

_____

_____

Please contact the person overleaf or our office if you are unable to attend

The Court, High Lane, Stockport SK6 8DX.
Telephone: Disley (0663) 65115

BUSINESS & MARKET RESEARCH PLC

BUSINESS & MARKET RESEARCH PLC

Registered Office as above   Registered No. 1138270 (England)

143

may be regarded as a nuisance call. It is even more important, therefore, to push for a commitment even to the point of discouraging the lukewarm.

The initial telephone recruitment must be followed up with a written invitation confirming the date, time and place, as illustrated in the example on page 143:

A telephone call 'to check you received my invitation' provides a means of further reinforcement, followed by another call on the day of the group.

Bearing in mind that managers and similar people may have fuller diaries than the average consumer, a longer recruitment timetable is desirable – two weeks rather than a few days. Three weeks, however, is about the maximum gap between recruitment and the date of the group. If any longer is left, this appears to be counter-productive; the date is 'forgotten' or other, more important things sidetrack the respondent.

Allow for a drop-out factor in business-to-business groups.

However thorough the recruitment work, attendance at business-to-business groups is more uncertain than in consumer research and a drop-out factor has to be allowed for. This varies according to the type of respondent involved, but as a rough rule, 15 or more firm promises of attendance at the first contact may drop to 10 or 12 on recontact after the written invitation has been received, with the eight sought actually turning up.

3. Leading groups

Although not essential, it is useful to have a helper or hostess available to assist the group leader. Such a person can take care of the mundane but important tasks such as making sure the refreshments are there when required, solving panics such as two pieces of equipment to plug in one socket and welcoming respondents. The leader may prefer to limit contact with the group before the meeting starts – this is a matter of personal preference. In any case, the leader should arrive in good time so that problems can be solved before respondents start arriving and, if the venue is an hotel, make sure the staff understand the arrangements.

It is best to keep refreshments simple and laid out for self-service. The meeting is meant to seem informal and waiter service is unnecessary.

Make sure the food and drink is available as respondents arrive and not brought in once the group has started.

The group leader's real work starts with the meeting. The major task is to ensure that everything important is covered in the discussion. As mentioned earlier, the topic checklist is only a guide and in a successful group the sequence will not be adhered to. For this reason, the group leader must be completely confident of the subject coverage and how important, to the overall objectives, each element is. The discussion must also be paced adequately with, where necessary, discussion of one topic, however interesting the comments, curtailed, so that other subjects are not left out entirely.

The leader must also think about his own attitudes to both the subject of the research and his role in the group. A group leader is a *facilitator*. He or she is there to encourage respondents to communicate their own views and feelings and, as far as is possible, not to influence the attitudes expressed. While the group leader is firmly in control of the group, this should not be forcibly apparent to respondents once the discussion starts. Above all, the group is not an ego trip for the group leader. The group has not gone well if, on listening to the recording, the leader is heard more than the respondents.

Generally, the first few minutes of the meeting determine how well the group 'works'. The important thing is to have *participation* and this should be made clear in the initial introduction.

The introduction is designed to remind the respondents who you are and who you work for, to reassure them (no matter what was said at the recruitment some will still expect the meeting to be a subtle sales ploy), to tell them what they are expected to do – talk – and very briefly to define the subject matter. The recording of the discussion is mentioned and for ethical reasons it has to be, but not in a way that invites objections. Group participation is then initiated by inviting everyone to say something in turn.

Techniques available to the leader, once the group starts, can be classified as either leader *initiatives* or *problem handling*. The simplest initiative for the group leader to use is the *direct question* – for example, 'Why would you think of taking out a personal pension scheme?' Much of the leader's input in a group will take the form of direct questions.

145

Phrase the question to produce a discursive response rather than just a 'yes' or 'no'. A problem in using direct questions is that they tend to lead to responses one by one rather than encouraging a discussion. This can be partly overcome by following up the initial response, as in the following example:

Leader: What are pension companies like?

Respondent: To me they are a lot of crooks.

Leader: You think pension companies are crooks. What about the rest of you? Do you feel this way?

It is bad practice to lead respondents.

In conventional interviewing, it is bad practice to lead respondents. With care, a group leader can appear to express an opinion as a means of developing the discussion. If, for example, the views expressed have been one sided, a *challenge* may enable other and less superficial attitudes to come out. For example: 'You all seem to have a low opinion of pension companies, yet you all have pensions and nobody has mentioned cases of people suffering because they took out a scheme.'

A similar technique is to ask the respondent to put forward a particular point of view. The one with the most negative view of pension companies is asked to think of some positive aspect. An extension of this is *role playing*. For example: 'I want you to imagine you are a pension salesperson. Pretend you are calling at a prospective customer's home for the first time. What would you say to him about the advantages of buying from your company?' Role playing can be extended to acting as well as talking. Someone might be asked to show how it feels to be a particular brand of a product. In this case, what is important is not so much what the particular respondent does, but the stimulus it gives to the discussion. Similarly, respondents can be asked to draw or even model in clay a particular aspect of a subject (for example, how they will look when they retire) and this is used to encourage subsequent discussion as well as providing a non-verbal record of attitudes. Another type of acting involves asking respondents to demonstrate how they use a product.

An important function of the group leader is to provide information.

An important role of the group leader is to give information. If the subject of a group is a new product concept, this must be adequately

146

presented to the respondents through concept sheets, showing illustrations or statements, in an easy-to-digest form.

The use of concept sheets is not limited to new product research. They play an important part in many groups and considerable thought and imagination need to be given to their design. The group leader can also use many other means for presenting information to respondents, including showing actual products, mock-ups, models and video presentations. However, one important consideration is that the presentation of any type of information must be carried out quickly and effectively, due to the limited time available. Otherwise, the discussion becomes a lecture, with little feedback from respondents.

Self-completion questionnaires can be used in a group for several purposes including: obtaining an indication of individual attitudes before the group discusses the subject, to give a record of responses that lends itself to more formal analysis than is possible by simply listening to the group and to provide factual data. In the latter case, respondents may be asked to complete the questionnaire before the group starts – this serves both to keep them occupied and saves having to use valuable discussion time to cover simple factual information. However useful, questionnaires must be regarded as an ancillary. There is no point in going to the trouble of recruiting a group and then having most of the time taken up completing questionnaires.

Every group has its problems and some are unique to particular groups and subjects. A few general problems and strategies for dealing with them are outlined in Table 6.1.

4. Analysing groups

The work needed after the group has been carried out is considerable and should not be skimped. Immediate debriefs, based only on the group leader's recall of what happened, is poor practice. The record of the meeting is a tape recording. In analysis, the contents of each tape have to be examined in detail and integrated with tapes from the other groups in the programme. A possible approach to this stage of group discussion research is as follows:

1. Transcribe the tapes in full. This is usually done by an audio-typist and, for best results, experience of working from group tapes is important.

Table 6.1 *Group problems and dealing with them*

Problem	Solution
Non-talkative group	Make sure the group knows they are expected to talk.
	Allay suspicions and doubts about the purpose of the group.
	Try different stimuli: questions, challenges, having them draw, etc.
	Change the topic.
Non-talkative member	Ask member questions or seek comments on other contributions.
Domineering member	Encourage others to talk as well or instead.
	Thank member and ask others for their opinion.
The joker	Show no reaction to the jokes.
The side-tracked group	Change the topic and bring back to the point.

2. Listen to the tapes while reading the transcriptions and mark additional comments.
3. Read through the transcripts and highlight the important comments and categorise them by subject – a simple coding system may be used.
4. Integrate comments on the same subject from the different tapes. Cut and paste is one way to do this – either physically or by using a word-processing package.
5. Plan a structure to the final report and rearrange the material from step 4 accordingly.

The process of group discussion analysis involves, to a large extent, testing various hypotheses developed about the subject against what was

Perhaps you need less when you retire.......

Some believe that less income is needed on retirement. Reasons for believing this include a view of retirement as a time of inaction and passivity. Also, it may be thought that on retirement most material wants have been met (and presumably will not recur).

> "When you retire you just sit around bored so you don't need much to spend."

> "Pensioners don't need as much."

> "And hopefully we will have arrived at this comfortable state where we won't need much because we will already have most things we need. Obviously you will have more leisure time, more holidays but in other respects you won't need money."

.......**But you may need as much or more**.

Such views were by no means universal amongst our respondents. Acquisitiveness, it was said, did not always decline with age.

> "Gosh I don't know how you can say that. I mean looking at people I know who have retired, their lifestyles haven't changed at all. They still want, want, want. It's unbelievable."

Also, in some respects, requirements in old age might be greater rather than less. This particularly applied in health care; another area where future government provision could not be taken for granted.

> "Also, the way things are going, you are expected to pay for more and more of your health care, you might need more money not less. When you are old you will be bound to reach a stage when health care is needed and you might have to pay to get it."

29

actually said in the discussion. The hypothesis may have arisen out of the discussion itself or have been formed at the planning stage.

Group discussion work inevitably has a subjective element; the results are bound to some extent to reflect the interests of the researcher involved and this must be accepted by both the researcher and whoever uses the results. A professional researcher, however, recognises this problem and takes care that, although subjectivity is inevitable, the results presented are still grounded in what actually happened in the group.

A specimen page from a report on group discussion research is shown on page 149. This example shows how verbatim quotations from the groups are used to illustrate general themes.

Hall tests

Material suitable for hall tests includes products, packs and advertising material.

The purpose of hall tests is to obtain the attitudes of a statistically valid sample to whatever is tested in the 'hall'. Generally, the respondents brought into the hall are recruited in the immediate location with quotas used to obtain a representative sample. Hall tests are more expansive than street interviews and are used because the test material cannot be practically carried round and shown in the course of normal interviews.

The material shown in hall tests can include:

- *Products*, particularly foods of all types. Almost any product can be considered, providing it can be shown or used in a realistic way. It is clearly impractical to ask respondents to try out shampoo in a hall although they could give opinions based on the product's appearance and smell. Product testing of this sort is often part of new product development.
- *Packs*. Often a product is distinguished by its pack rather than its contents. Testing acceptance of pack designs is an important research requirement.
- *Advertising material*. Although some types of advertising material can be shown in the street or home, it may be more practical to set up displays in a hall.

Business-to-business products can also be researched through the hall test approach. In this case, however, recruitment is by telephone and respondents have to be drawn from a much wider area. Once in the hall, respondents also generally stay longer. The products shown may be large – for example, commercial vehicles. The term *clinic* is used for this type of hall test.

1. Product testing

We now consider some general principles of product testing in halls. The approach in home placement (often used where the product cannot be practically tested in a hall) is broadly the same.

In the hall, the respondent is asked to look at, handle and use (for example, eat) the product. At appropriate points in the test, questions are asked to establish attitudes to and acceptance of the product. Usually, the test is designed to provide comparisons between two or more products. If a new product is being tested, comparisons may be with the brand leader.

Product testing can be *blind* or *branded*. In blind product testing, the respondents do not know the brand of products being tested and, therefore, attitudes are based on experience of the product only, and not influenced by the brand identity (the 'halo' or 'horns' effect). Most product testing is blind although there may be good reasons to show the brand, perhaps in the later stages of the test.

Product testing can be blind or branded.

Multiple rather than *monadic* testing is more common. In multiple testing, each respondent tests in turn two, three or more products and gives responses for each. In monadic testing, each respondent tests only one product and comparisons are made by having the different products tested by matched samples. This is clearly more expensive. If it is decided that a sample size of 200 is needed to provide reliable data, two samples of 200, rather than one, are required for monadic testing of two products. There is also a problem of ensuring that the samples are matched sufficiently to allow meaningful comparisons. Arguably, however, monadic testing more accurately mirrors real consumption; in everyday life, we do not eat different brands of chocolate in immediate succession to decide which we prefer. Also, multiple testing is not practical for some products (for example, strong mint sweets).

Monadic testing more accurately mirrors real consumption.

Because hall tests are a quantitative method, sample size is important in planning such tests. It is important to be confident that any differences

Table 6.2 *Significance of paired comparison*

Sample size	% Minimum significant difference
100	20
200	14
300	11
400	10
500	9
1000	6

found in responses reflect a real discrimination and not just a sampling error. Table 6.2 shows approximately, for different sample sizes, the level of difference in results between two products which can be regarded as statistically significant at 5 per cent probability.

If, among a sample of 300, we found that 55 per cent prefer product A and 45 per cent prefer product B, the difference in preference is 10 percentage points. From Table 6.2, you can see that for a sample of 300, the minimum difference that is statistically significant, at 5 per cent probability, is 11 per cent; therefore, the actual 10 per cent difference is not significant. In other words, there is more than a 1 in 20 chance (that is, 5 per cent probability) that the difference is just random.

As a general rule, reliable product testing requires samples of several hundred, although the total sample may be the aggregation of smaller numbers covered in several separate halls.

Quota sampling is nearly always used in hall tests. Quotas are set to provide a sample representative of the target market for the product being tested. The quotas may, therefore, be in terms of demographics (for example, housewives with children under 12 in social classes C1 and C2) and product behaviour (for example, people who bought sausages in the last month).

Product testing can be carried out at one venue alone, but obviously the sample is then restricted to one area. To allow for local or regional variations in attitudes, it is generally better to use several locations. A drawback to hall tests is that it is seldom practical to use more than a few venues for a test and, therefore, the geographical spread of the sample is inevitably restricted.

2. Planning a hall test

The critical steps in planning a hall test are as follows:

1. Decide sample size, number and broad location of venues, and set respondent quotas.
2. Find suitable venues.
3. Estimate daily respondent throughput at the venues and book for the required number of days.
4. Book interviewing and other staff required.
5. Plan how the products are to be presented in the tests.
6. Prepare questionnaires and other interviewer material.

A specimen planning sheet is provided in Figure 6.4.

Since respondents are normally recruited in the immediate vicinity of the halls, the most important consideration in the choice of a venue is its siting. The actual premises used can be a church hall, assembly rooms, nightclub or an empty shop. It must, however, be in or near a major shopping area. Because 'captured' respondents are normally escorted from wherever they are approached into the hall, a main street frontage is not critical but access should be reasonable and not up narrow stairs (this is also important when setting up the hall and taking in products). The venue size must be large enough for the envisaged throughput; in contrast to rooms used for group discussions, the venue can be quite a bit larger than is really needed.

The siting of the venue is the most important consideration.

Furniture and fittings required at a hall are seldom elaborate. Tables and chairs are needed to seat respondents and interviewers, and display products, screens may be necessary to separate different batches of respondents and kitchen facilities may be required to prepare the product for testing (or make refreshments for respondents or staff). These requirements cover most needs.

The throughput that can be achieved in a hall depends on staffing levels and the availability of potential respondents. It is clearly difficult to take 100 respondents through the hall in a day if relatively few people are about outside the hall. The quotas used are also relevant. Tight and restrictive quotas will make it harder to locate qualified respondents and

The throughput depends on staffing levels and the availability of potential respondents.

153

Job no: _____   **Product/Material:** _____

Total sample required: [   ]

Venues	Average no respondents	No of days	Dates booked
1. _____	_____	_____	_____ to _____
2. _____	_____	_____	_____ to _____
3. _____	_____	_____	_____ to _____
4. _____	_____	_____	_____ to _____

Staff	Venue 1	Venue 2	Venue 3	Venue 4
Supervisor	_____	_____	_____	_____
Interviewers	_____	_____	_____	_____
	_____	_____	_____	_____
	_____	_____	_____	_____
Helpers	_____	_____	_____	_____
	_____	_____	_____	_____

Product delivery arrangements:

_____

_____

Product preparation and display requirements:

_____

_____

Questionnaires to be ready by: _____ (Date)

And delivered to venues by: _____ (Date)

Figure 6.4 *Hall test planning sheet*

will, therefore, reduce throughput. The implications of staffing levels on throughput are considered later.

The products to be tested must be available in the right form, on the hall days. The product that is the objective of the research will normally come from the factory or warehouse. Comparison products must be bought in. If perishable foods are involved, the delivery logistics and storage facilities must be adequate to ensure that the products are tested in a good and safe condition. Where the product has to be prepared on site (diluted, cooked, etc.), standards have to be set to ensure each batch is the same. Blind testing may require ingenuity in erasing brand names and a labelling system will be needed to identify the products. In comparative testing, the order in which products are tried may significantly affect responses and such *order bias* is controlled by a strict procedure to rotate the order of presentation.

The general principles of questionnaire design obviously apply in hall tests as much as in other fieldwork. Questionnaires are normally structured, although open-ended questions may be included (for example, to probe reasons for a preference). The sequence of the questions must be linked to the way the product is shown, with interviewer instructions included to ensure a standard approach (respondents may be asked to give opinions based on appearance alone and only then asked to taste each product in turn). A recruitment questionnaire is used to control the sample and often this forms the front part of the full questionnaire. Part of a hall test questionnaire is provided, as an example, in Figure 6.5.

3. Running a hall test
The best method of using hall test staff is for each interviewer to go into the streets near the hall, approach potential respondents, go through the recruitment questions and persuade the respondent to spare the short time needed to take part in the hall test. The 'captive' is then brought into the hall and interviewed by the same member of staff. Where the team is split between recruiters and inside interviewers, there are often problems of either having nothing to do in the hall or being overwhelmed by a sudden rush.

Respondents are often offered a drink and biscuits in the hall (little more is needed in the way of incentives), so a few helpers may be needed to organise this and prepare products. The whole team needs managing

Respondent no: _____

Display Code IM

Code as applicable, 1st display 1
2nd display 2

Q5a I'd like you to consider this display of tinned meats. Thinking only about the packaging, as opposed to the type of meat or the manufacturer, which of these pack designs do you find most appealing? You will see from the display that there are 3 tin shapes for each design.

Q5b And which would be your second choice?

	Q5a 1st choice		Q5b 2nd choice
• Celebrity IM	1	Q6a	1
• Princes	2	Q6b	2
• Plumrose	3	Q6c	3

Q6a (ASK IF CELEBRITY IM IS THE FIRST CHOICE AT Q5A.) What is it about this design that makes you prefer it? (PROBE FULLY: Anything else?)

_____

_____

Q6b (ASK IF PRINCES IS THE FIRST CHOICE AT Q5A.) What is it about this design that makes you prefer it? (PROBE FULLY: Anything else?)

_____

_____

Q6c (ASK IF PLUMROSE IS THE FIRST CHOICE AT Q5A.) What is it about this design that makes you prefer it? (PROBE FULLY: Anything else?)

_____

_____

Q7a (ASK ALL.) Do you prefer this design (1st choice at Q5a) for all the three different tin shapes?
- Yes   1   Q8
- No   2   Q7b

Q7b For which tin shape don't you like this design?
- Small (chopped H & M)   1
- Medium (luncheon meat)   2
- Large (1lb ham)   3

Q7c Why do you say that? (PROBE: Any other reasons?)

_____

_____

Q8 (ASK ALL.) I am now going to read out some statements about the three tin designs on the display. For each I want you to tell me which, if any, of the designs the statements apply to. Firstly, which of the packs would you describe as being . . . (ROTATE ORDER, TICK, START MAKING SURE YOU GO BACK TO THE TOP AND READ OUT ALL THE STATEMENTS.)

		Celebrity IM	Princes	Plumrose	None
(a)	An attractive pack	1	2	3	4
(b)	An expensive pack	1	2	3	4
(c)	A modern pack	1	2	3	4
(d)	A value-for-money pack	1	2	3	4
(e)	A traditional pack	1	2	3	4
(f)	A pack containing a product you would feel happy giving to children	1	2	3	4
(g)	A cheap pack	1	2	3	4
(h)	A pack with appealing colours	1	2	3	4
(i)	A good quality pack	1	2	3	4
(j)	An appetising pack	1	2	3	4
(k)	An old-fashioned pack	1	2	3	4

(l)	A pack containing a healthy product	1	2	3	4
(m)	A pack that stands out	1	2	3	4
(n)	A pack containing a fresh product	1	2	3	4
(o)	An ordinary pack	1	2	3	4
(p)	A pack containing a good quality product	1	2	3	4

Q9 (SHOWCARD B.) I would now like you to choose a phrase from this card to tell me how much you like each of these pack designs. Remember, we are only interested in the design of the packaging so please concentrate on this.

Firstly for . . . how much do you like the design of their packaging? (ROTATE ORDER OF PACK DESIGNS BUT MAKE SURE YOU ASK ABOUT ALL 3 BRANDS.)

	Celebrity IM	Princes	Plumrose
• Liked it a lot	1	1	1
• Liked it a little	2	2	2
• Neither liked nor disliked it	3	3	3
• Disliked it a little	4	4	4
• Disliked it a lot	5	5	5

Figure 6.5 *Specimen hall test questionnaire*

and someone in charge should be there all day. If timetables are really tight, it may be possible to have staff at the hall to carry out some or all of the data processing required.

On the first day of the test, time will be needed to set up furniture, arrange products, and so on. Also, the interviewing team must be briefed.

The productivity of the hall team will depend on several factors, including the interview length, the time taken in trying products, the type of respondents sought and the pedestrian volumes near the hall. If we assume that the product test and interview can be carried out in 15 minutes, then each interviewer might need about the same length of time again to recruit each respondent (with more or less time needed depending on the quotas to be met and pedestrian volumes). Each interviewer would, therefore, process two respondents an hour and, working six hours, 12 per day. On this basis, a team of ten interviewers could cover 100 respondents per day, but unless the hall was in a major city, pedestrian volumes might be too small to support this number of interviewers working at once. However, with this sort of calculation, a reasonable estimate of hall throughput can be made at the planning stage.

Clinics

Clinics are usually a major, expensive research project requiring detailed planning. Full coverage of this rather specialist type of market research cannot be attempted here. We will, however, briefly highlight some of the key differences between halls and clinics.

1. Venue
The nature of the products being shown may be a very restrictive factor in choosing a venue. A case in point is commercial vehicle clinics. Relatively few venues are large enough or have the right access to accommodate large trucks.

Another aspect of venue choice is that respondents generally find their own way there and, therefore, the site must be easy to find and with adequate parking.

2. Recruitment
In business-to-business clinic research, recruitment is normally by telephone, with potential respondents contacted at their place of work. Although the numbers of respondents sought are much larger, the process is much the same as recruiting for business-to-business groups. The catchment area, over which recruitment is carried out, is often practically restricted to about 25 miles or half an hour's travel, and in planning the research, the likely numbers of potential respondents available in the catchment must be considered. It is clearly not possible to recruit 100 respondents if there are fewer than 1000 people in the area who qualify for inclusion in the sample. Even with a written invitation

159

and reminder calls following the recruitment, some drop-out must be anticipated and allowed for. Perhaps 25 to 40 per cent of those giving the firmest assurances will not turn up for the event.

Clinic respondents need to be offered reasonable tangible incentives: food and drink at the venue and a 'take away' such as a bottle of spirits. With 100 or more respondents, the incentive costs are not inconsequential.

3. Running the clinic

Recruitment is a major effort and expense; however, once brought into the clinic, respondents are usually interviewed in more depth than in hall tests. Administered interviewing and self-completion sheets may be used in combination. At the end of the formal interview, some respondents may also be asked to participate in mini group discussions.

◀ CHAPTER 7 ▶

DATA ANALYSIS

This chapter is about the analysis of questionnaires. We cover the output sought from data analysis including some different ways of analysing information, and the special requirements of open-ended questions and numeric data. Then we describe the various methods and tools available for carrying out data analysis.

Data analysis output

1. Different ways of analysing information

In the analysis of questionnaires, the responses of individual respondents are generally of no interest in themselves. Rather, the aim is to be able to make *generalisations* about all or part of the sample. If the sample is truly representative, it is then possible to extrapolate the results to the whole population.

We will illustrate the type of output commonly sought in data analysis by taking, as an example, just one question from a survey:

Q5 How likely are you to buy the appliance in the next two years?
(PROMPT AS BELOW. ONE RESPONSE ONLY.)
- Very likely   ( )
- Fairly likely   ( )
- Neither likely/unlikely   ( )
- Fairly unlikely   ( )
- Very unlikely   ( )

Table 7.1 *Likelihood of buying appliance in the next two years (all respondents)*

Likelihood of buying	Percentage
Very likely	25
Fairly likely	40
Neither likely/unlikely	14
Fairly unlikely	18
Very unlikely	3
Total	**100**
Sample size	200

This question is closed and pre-coded; all the possible response options are shown on the questionnaire and the respondent is asked to select just one to indicate his or her personal likelihood of purchase.

Table 7.1 shows a simple analysis of this question. The interview sample was 200. The data from the question is shown in percentages rather than absolute numbers. However, the sample size shows how many respondents are involved and this is important in making any inferences from the table. As will be recalled from earlier chapters, the size of a sample has an effect on sampling error; therefore, the smaller the sample size, the more cautiously we should treat the data. For this reason, all tables of this sort (and as we will see shortly, all columns in a table) *must* include sample sizes.

In analysing data, it is important to know the sample size.

Tables must also be descriptive with adequate titles and labelling of each response; if read in isolation, the table should be understandable. You will notice that in the previous table 'all respondents' were included. We may, however, wish to show the responses of just part of the sample – in other words, use a *filter*. Table 7.2 shows the likelihood of purchase, not of the whole sample, but just for those who already own the appliance (a separate question established ownership). The use of a filter in the analysis is clearly stated and the sample size now falls to 100 (100 out of the total sample are appliance owners). Filtering is used for questions not asked of all respondents – for example, we may only ask existing owners the question about future purchase. In this case, because some respondents did not give any response, the column would not add up to 100 per cent without the use of a filter.

Table 7.2 *Likelihood of buying the appliance in the next two years (existing owners of the appliance)*

Likelihood of buying	Percentage
Very likely	40
Fairly likely	0
Neither likely/unlikely	25
Fairly unlikely	30
Very unlikely	5
Total	**100**
Sample size	100

Instead of showing separate data for appliance owners, we may wish to have a table that compares the likelihood of purchase for owners *and* non-owners (we now assume that both owners and non-owners were asked about the likelihood of purchase). In Table 7.3, the likelihood of purchase is, therefore, *cross-analysed* by ownership (this is indicated in the table title). The total column is still retained but sample sizes are shown for each cross-break column. The table reverts to 'all respondents' – there is no longer a filter although filters and cross-analysis can be used

Table 7.3 *Likelihood of buying the appliance in the next two years by existing ownership of the appliance (respondents)*

Likelihood of buying	Total %	Owners %	Non-owners %
Very likely	25	40	10
Fairly likely	40	0	80
Neither likely/unlikely	15	25	5
Fairly unlikely	18	30	5
Very unlikely	3	5	0
Total	**100**	**100**	**100**
Sample size	200	100	100

in combination; the same table format could be repeated, but using a filter just for owner occupiers and excluding tenants.

Showing the sample size for each cross-break column is important in table interpretation. In Table 7.3, 40 per cent of owners but only 10 per cent of non-owners are 'very likely' to purchase; therefore, we may infer that owners generally are very much more likely to buy. However, this assumes that the difference between owners and non-owners is real and not just within the range of sampling error. Any judgement requires the sample sizes – the size of the subsamples – to be known so that the statistical significance of the difference between the results can be calculated. (Table 6.2 provides a rough and ready indication of significance; for example, with samples of 100 a 30 per cent difference is significant at 5 per cent probability.) In practice, the sample sizes involved in cross-analysis are often disregarded, with the consequence that conclusions are based on wholly unreliable data.

The cross-break used in our example is simple – owners *vs* non-owners only. Obviously, the breaks can be much more elaborate with cross-analysis by more than one question and more variables for each question. Compound cross-breaks can also be used – for example, to compare the responses of owner occupiers and tenants separately for both appliance owners and non-owners:

Total	Appliance owners		Appliance non-owners	
	Owner occupiers	Tenants	Owner occupiers	Tenants
	%	%	%	%

Responses to scalar questions (our question about likelihood of purchase is a scalar question) are often summarised as *mean scores*; that is, the responses are given numeric values and the mean score is the weighted average of these values, taking into account the numbers giving each response. In the following example, shown in Table 7.4, the responses are given numeric values ranging from +2 to –2 and the mean scores calculated are shown immediately above the sample size at the foot of each column. We can, therefore, make easy comparisons, using just one value, of the likelihood of purchase among the total sample, owners and non-owners.

Table 7.4   *Likelihood of buying appliance in the next two years by existing ownership of the*
appliance (all respondents)

Likelihood of buying	Total %	Owners %	Non-owners %
Very likely (+2)	25	40	10
Fairly likely (+1)	40	0	80
Neither likely/unlikely (0)	14	25	5
Fairly unlikely (−1)	18	30	5
Very unlikely (−2)	3	5	0
Total	**100**	**100**	**100**
Mean score	*+0.66*	*+0.40*	*+0.95*
Sample size	200	100	100

In Table 7.4, a comparison of the mean score values for owners and non-owners suggests that non-owners are rather more likely to purchase (a positive value of 0.95 compared to only 0.40). This, however, provides a clear example of the limitations and dangers of using mean scores. The table indicates that 40 per cent of owners and only 10 per cent of non-owners are 'very likely' to purchase, but the implications of this have to be weighed against the further 80 per cent of non-owners who are 'fairly likely' to purchase and the 0 per cent of owners in this category. Some judgement (perhaps based on comparisons with other surveys) will have to be made about how the responses are likely to be translated into actual behaviour. The key point is that mean scores can mislead by over-simplifying.

Mean scores can mislead results by over-simplifying.

Incidentally, the values attributed to the responses in Table 7.4 are either arbitrary or based on our beliefs about how much more likely the 'very likely' respondents are to buy than the 'fairly likely'. We could assign values of +3 to 'very likely' and +1 to 'fairly likely', and in this case the mean score values would change to 0.80 for owners and 1.05 for non-owners. With other values, owners would have the higher mean score. This is perfectly legitimate, although in practice it is rare to use response values with unequal intervals (such as +3 and +1).

At one time, calculation of mean scores was laborious and, therefore, used sparingly by researchers. Today, with the aid of computers, mean scores can be calculated as a matter of course. However, the true implications of responses can be hidden by the pseudo-sophistication of quite spurious mean scores – shown to two decimal places. Quite apart from other considerations, it should be remembered that the principles of statistical significance apply just as much to mean scores as percentage differences, and mean scores of, say, 1.10 and 0.91 may not indicate statistically significant differences.

On the whole, it is better *not* to use mean scores, but instead to interpret the actual distribution of scale responses, even though it involves more work.

At the data analysis stage, *weighting* can be used to correct a sample that under- or over-represents certain groups within a population (this was mentioned in Chapter 3). In Table 7.5, it can be seen that 43 per cent of a sample own the appliance and that ownership is higher among owner occupiers (60 per cent) than tenants (25 per cent). However, the bottom two rows of the table (which add across) show that owner occupiers are under-represented in the sample – only 50 per cent of the sample are in this category compared to a known 75 per cent among the whole population. Since the ownership level is higher among owner occupiers than tenants, we can assume that the total figure under-estimates overall ownership.

Weighting can be used to correct a sample that either under- or over-represents certain groups within a population.

By weighting, we can estimate what the total ownership level would

Table 7.5   *Ownership of the appliance by home tenure (all respondents)*

Own appliance	Total %	Owner occupiers %	Tenants %
Yes	43	60	25
No	57	40	75
Total	**100**	**100**	**100**
Sample size	200	100	100
Sample (% across)	100	50	50
Population (% across)	100	75	25

Table 7.6 *Ownership of the appliance by home tenure: weighted totals (all respondents)*

| Own appliance | Total | | Owner occupiers | Tenants |
	Unweighted	Weighted	%	%
Yes	43	51	60	25
No	57	49	40	75
Total	**100**	**100**	**100**	**100**
Sample size	200	200	100	100
Sample (% across)		100	50	50
Population (% across)		100	75	25
Weighting factor			1.50	0.50

have been if the sample *had* been representative. Table 7.6 shows the weighted values for total ownership. The weighting factors used are the sample proportions for owner occupiers or tenants divided into the corresponding proportions in the whole population. The weighted totals are calculated by multiplying the ownership levels among owner occupiers and tenants by the appropriate weighting factor, adding the results together and expressing the value as a percentage.

In our example, the weighting calculation was easily carried out. In practice, with more complex and numerous tables, the work is very laborious. Furthermore, weighting may take account of several rather than just one sample characteristic. For these reasons, the procedure is not often attempted without using a computer analysis package that includes weighting as a standard function.

2. Open-ended questions

Up to this point, we have only considered the analysis of closed and pre-coded questions. The analysis of open-ended questions introduces the additional problem of *coding*. The following question was asked of 100 respondents (those not expecting to buy the appliance) and the responses were recorded verbatim by the interviewers. If all the responses were listed in full, we could have 100 different statements (although some differences would be slight). Just the first nine responses to the question are listed.

The analysis of open-ended questions introduces the additional problem of coding.

167

Q5 Why would you not consider buying this appliance in the next two years? (DO NOT PROMPT. RECORD VERBATIM.)

Respondent	Response
1.	They are too big to fit in my kitchen.
2.	I cannot afford to buy.
3.	They are ugly looking things.
4.	I don't like the colours and they cost too much.
5.	I hear they are unreliable.
6.	With just the two of us, we don't need one now.
7.	I am waiting until they come down in price.
8.	They are too difficult to use.
9.	I don't know really.

With only the nine responses shown, it is not that easy, just by reading through the list, to make any generalisations about the reasons for non-purchase. Looking at all 100 responses makes matters even worse. What we need to do is to group the individual responses into categories that we judge to have a similar meaning. We can designate each group with a number which, if the data was to be computer processed, would be the input codes used in data entry.

An appropriate grouping of the nine responses is shown in Table 7.7. Note that response 4 above is a *multi-response* in the sense that two reasons are given in the one statement; and, in the grouping, response 4 in fact appears in two separate categories.

Assuming that all 100 responses can be sensibly classified into the five categories listed, the results from our analysis of the questionnaires might be as shown in Table 7.8. Because of multi-responses (two or more

Table 7.7 *Grouping of responses*

Code	Response category	Responses included
1	Design of appliance	1, 3, 4, 8
2	Cost factors	2, 4, 7
3	Unreliability of appliance	5
4	Have no need for appliance	6
5	Don't know	9

Table 7.8 *Reasons for not considering buying the appliance (those not considering buying)*

Reason	Percentage
Design of appliance	35
Cost factors	25
Unreliability of appliance	21
Have no need for appliance	18
Don't know	10
Total	*

* Multi-responses and therefore the column does not total 100.

reasons given by one respondent), the column totals more than 100 per cent. Conventionally, this is indicated in the manner shown; what the total of the column actually adds up to is of no real interest. Tables of data from open-ended questions can include filters and cross-analysis in just the same way as closed and pre-coded questions. Obviously, mean scores are not relevant.

The way in which we have grouped the first nine responses to the question is to some extent arbitrary. We have, for example, grouped the following four responses under one category:

Design of appliance
1. They are too big to fit in my kitchen.
3. They are ugly looking things.
4. I don't like the colours (and they cost too much).
8. They are too difficult to use.

However, such grouping may mask some quite important differences in response. Out of the 100 responses, it is possible that the major negative aspect of design is in fact the size of the appliance. Marketing staff using the research would have some positive guidance on product redesign if this was brought out in the research findings. For the 100 responses, therefore, dozens of different groupings or *coding frames* could be devised. None in isolation is necessarily better or worse but one or two would prove more *useful* to the report writer and research user. The analysis of open-ended questions, therefore, calls for considerable judgement and is not mechanical in the way that pre-coded question analysis is.

Some practical aspects of the coding of open-ended questions are referred to again, later in this chapter.

Numeric responses

Some questions seek a numeric value as the response. For example:

Q8 How much did you pay for this appliance? (RECORD ACTUAL VALUE. IF NECESSARY, GIVE RESPONDENT TIME TO CHECK.)

$$£ \underline{\hspace{3cm}}$$

The resulting responses can be listed and then classified into appropriate intervals, as shown in Table 7.9. Notice that the intervals are not equally spaced; this has been done deliberately to show that most consumers pay in the narrow range of £340 to £345. We could have pre-coded the questionnaire with what we *believed* were appropriate intervals, but there is a danger that we might have chosen them badly; for example, under £250, £250–£300, £300–£350 and over £350, with the result that 86 per cent of the responses would have been in the £300–£350 interval. For this reason, interval setting at the coding stage may be preferred (it may, however, be easier to obtain responses if pre-coded intervals can be used as interview prompts).

Numeric data can also be analysed in other ways. In business-to-business research, in particular, we may wish to express a range of values

Table 7.9 *Amount paid for appliance (those who have bought the appliance in last two years)*

Amount paid £	Percentage
Under 300	3
Over 301–340	19
Over 340–345	54
Over 345–350	13
Over 350	7
Don't know/can't remember	4
Total	**100**
Sample size	58

by a number of statistical functions. The values from the sample (or sample strata) might then be *grossed up* to provide estimates of the whole population.

Planning the analysis at the questionnaire stage

Before moving on to discuss how data analysis can be carried out in practice, it is worth making the important point that analysis planning must start at the questionnaire design stage – you *cannot* analyse what you do not ask. We may, for example, decide that ownership of the appliance ought to be cross-analysed by car ownership. This is fine as long as the questionnaire covered car ownership. If it did not, there is nothing we can do apart from recontacting the sample and asking the supplementary question, which is a difficult and expensive task.

Analysis planning must start at the questionnaire design stage.

Methods of data analysis

The methods or tools available for questionnaire data analysis include:

- Hand or manual analysis
- Using general-purpose computer software
- Using specialised survey analysis software
- Putting the work out to a computer bureau

Each of these has its place and use.

At its simplest, hand analysis involves counting the responses to a question. We can either sort the questionnaires into piles corresponding to each response or use a simple checking sheet, such as the following:

Q5 Ownership of the appliance:

- Yes   HHl HHl HHl HHl HHl HHl HHl HHl

                                          Total 40

- No   HHl HHl HHl HHl HHl HHl HHl HHl
       HHl HHl HHl HHl

                                            Total 60

Although the task is laborious, it is quite possible to produce either filtered or cross-analysis tables by hand analysis. In the case of cross-

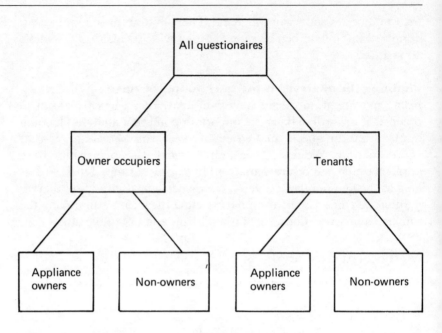

Figure 7.1 *Sorting questionnaires for cross-analysis*

analysis, we would, for example, first sort the questionnaires between owner occupiers and tenants, and then sort these two piles between owners and non-owners of the appliance (computers do exactly the same, but electronically). This would enable us to prepare a table of ownership by tenure (see Figure 7.1).

The manual analysis of open-ended questions can involve either simply reading each response and writing down relevant categories as you go along (ticking those you have listed as they crop up again), or going through a separate coding stage and marking each response with a relevant code. The latter approach is better (since you have a record of how each response has been categorised) and essential if any sort of cross-analysis is to be attempted.

Data logging sheets are useful in manual analysis. Another approach to manual analysis is to use a *data logging sheet*. The responses from all (or key) questions are transferred to the sheet, where columns are used for the questions and rows for each questionnaire. Such sheets can be particularly useful for analysing the sort of numeric often covered in business-to-business research. Columns can be totalled, averaged and easily adjusted if errors are found or changes need to be

Table 7.10   *Data logging sheet*

	Question						
	Q1				Q2	Q3	
Respondent company	*Types of metal component bought*				*Annual component consumption*	*Supply sources*	
	Steel	*Copper*	*Alum*	*Other*	*£000*	*In-house*	*Outside*
1. F G Adern	x	x			5	x	
2. Elbo Co		x			1	x	
3. Andrew WS			x		4		x
4. Express		x			12	x	

made. Furthermore, it is possible to search for simple relationships between different variables/question responses; for example, in Table 7.10, do those with an in-house supply source have, on average, a larger or smaller consumption level?

If you use data logging sheets, you must write neatly and legibly. If you are not capable of this, get someone else to do the work or use a computer.

Nowadays, hand analysis is only used for small-scale sample analysis. In most commercial organisations, it is cheaper as well as quicker to use computer data processing, or possibly to put the work out, once the volume of data exceeds a certain level.

Most offices are now equipped with a micro-computer or PC and some of the general-purpose software packaged with the PC can be adapted for data analysis. The best example of this is the *spreadsheet*. Instead of recording data on to a handwritten logging sheet, a spreadsheet can be set up. Not only is the work much neater but various automatic calculations and sorting features can be used. If, for example, we need to change the steel consumption of one company, the totals will be automatically adjusted. Similarly, we could array the companies in order of consumption. The spreadsheet also reduces some of the tedium – for example, converting responses given in the form of percentage breakdowns into absolute values. Spreadsheets can also be used to carry out weighting or other manipulations of data.

Using a spreadsheet programme reduces the tedium of calculations.

Database software is also adaptable as a market research analysis tool, making it possible to carry out quite sophisticated filtering or cross-analysis.

A market research department will eventually consider buying special-purpose software developed for survey analysis. There are quite a few packages available to work on standard PCs. Costs vary from a few hundred pounds up to several thousand at the time of writing. We cannot review here what is available or advise you what to buy. A general principle is, however, that there is a trade-off between *user friendliness* and *flexibility/sophistication*. Packages that are easy to use tend to be inflexible (will not allow you to decide the form of the table presentation) and unsophisticated (weighting may not be built in). Packages that are flexible may call for considerable training in their use and so are often only accessible to specialists. If your need is modest and intermittent, it will not be worth getting to grips with a sophisticated package and it will be uneconomic to employ any expert help. The process of using an in-house computer with purpose built software will be discussed later.

Consider contracting the data analysis work to specialist bureaux. There is much to be said for putting data analysis out to one of the bureaux that specialise in this sort of work. Such specialists have the hardware, software and, above all, expertise. They also produce high-quality table output. If you decide on this approach, it is important to speak to the bureau's staff at the questionnaire design stage to find out their requirements in terms of data recording. Most bureaux input data in *punch-card format* (actual punch cards are no longer used). Each 'card' has 80 columns and each column can record (as a single or multi-punch) up to 12 response codes. Responses from the questionnaire are coded in this columnar format and input in this form. In the example, the interviewer circles the appropriate code and this is input under column 12 (indicated by the number in brackets). Each 'card' carries a questionnaire identification number and if more than one card is needed per questionnaire, a card number as well. A questionnaire number or other numeric data is recorded with one column assigned per digit.

Computer packages for use in-house also require data to be recorded in a certain format, either punch-card or using strict question numbering conventions. With input work involving numeric codes, questions are best laid out so that the interviewer circles relevant codes.

Q5 How likely are you to buy the appliance in the next two years?
(PROMPT AS BELOW. ONE RESPONSE ONLY.)

(12)

- Very likely   1
- Fairly likely   2
- Neither likely/unlikely   3
- Fairly unlikely   4
- Very unlikely   5

Although specialist bureaux can provide an excellent service, there are a number of disadvantages entailed:

- Coding of open-ended questions still has to be carried out, and usually this is done better in-house. Such coding is a major part of the whole data analysis process.
- Problems can arise from inadequate communication of requirements in terms of table specification to the bureau. Invariably this is the user's fault.
- It is not so easy to run off that extra table. However, tools such as the fax have reduced this sort of inflexibility.
- Using a bureau may seem quite expensive. However, the cost of setting up in-house facilities can be even higher.

The data analysis process

In this final section of the chapter, we outline the processes involved in in-house data analysis, using a small team equipped with specialist software on PCs. The process is much the same if a bureau is used, although some of the work is carried out on their premises rather than yours (see Figure 7.2).

1. Questionnaire editing

Questionnaire editing is the process of checking each completed questionnaire to identify problems arising from interviewer error in administration or recording (and, more seriously, errors in question-naire design which cannot now be rectified). Problems are flagged and either corrected by judgement or referred back to the interviewer. At worst, an arbitrary decision is made on how to treat an ambiguous or nil response – for example, we may add a 'not asked' or 'no response'

175

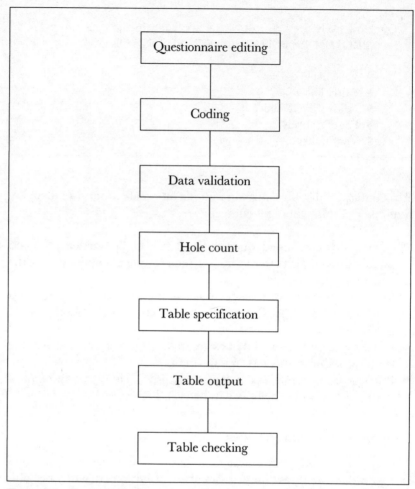

Figure 7.2 *Data analysis stages*

category. On the whole, such editing is best done by the manager of the field force rather than the data analysis team; if there are problems with interviewers' work, the field force manager should know what these are.

As a result of editing, all pre-coded and closed question responses should be in a state ready for data input.

2. Coding
Coding is the process of converting the responses from open-ended questions (and those with an open-ended element) into a form that can

be input into the computer. The general principles involved have already been discussed.

The first step is to develop a *coding frame*. If the number of questionnaires involved in the survey is 100 or less, each questionnaire is read and the coding frame developed (or a code may be developed as we go along, although this is not the ideal way of working). With larger surveys, a sample of the questionnaires is taken – at least 50, or 20 per cent, whichever is the larger, including some from a number of interviewers – and the coding frame is developed from these. An example of a coding frame is shown in Figure 7.3.

Some suggestions for developing a coding frame are:

● There should not be too many codes/response categories. If there are

Job no: 276/89C

Question no: 13B

Code	Description
1	Happy/satisfied with present heating
2	Can't afford it/too expensive
3	Don't like them/unattractive
4	Small/compact/don't take up too much room
5	Dislike gas/too dangerous/unsafe near children
6	Prefer gas/gas safer/gas cleaner
7	Controllable/can use when you need them
8	Already have them
9	No outside wall
10	Other
11	Don't know
12	No response

Figure 7.3 *Specimen coding frame*

10 or more, the resulting table is likely to be too complicated to show a general picture.

- Similarly, codes/categories that include only a few responses – under 5 per cent – are generally of no use. (There are exceptions to this rule.)
- Conversely, the 'other' or 'dustbin' category (where responses that do not seem to fit anywhere else are put) should not be more than about 10 per cent.
- When setting up the coding frame, it is sensible to allocate some standard codes to 'other', 'don't know' and 'can't remember' – e.g. 10, 11 and 12.

Once the coding frames for all the open-ended questions have been developed, coding itself can be carried out. Each response is read and a judgement made as to which code frame category it matches. The appropriate code is then written on to the questionnaire ready for data input.

Developing a coding frame requires skill and judgement.

The coding of open-ended questions is beset with problems and is often so badly done that it would have been far better to devise a closed question in the first place. In particular:

- Developing a coding frame requires considerable skill and judgement. The work can only be done well by the researcher responsible for the project and/or whoever will eventually write the report. Too often the task is delegated to someone who has no idea what the research is about and lacks the necessary skill.
- Making decisions on which code to use for each response also calls for judgement and skill. Research has shown that, in practice, errors in this part of the process are often greater than the interviewer or sampling error. The problem can be reduced, but not eradicated, through staff training and checking procedures.
- Coding can be a very expensive process. In some cases, the coding costs can be greater than the interviewing costs (especially in the case of telephone questionnaires with many open-ended questions).

In small sample research, it may be better for the data analysis team simply to list all verbatims from open-ended questions and let the researcher in charge build up a table from this source. In larger-scale research, a complete or partial list of verbatims may be passed to the researcher to be used in devising a coding frame. Incidentally, a practice to be discouraged is the inclusion of verbatim lists in final reports. This is ludicrous in the case of larger samples. The report is meant to simplify and generalise; it should not be padded out with long lists that nobody will ever read or digest.

In consumer research, a task that cuts across editing and coding is social class classification. At either the editing or coding stage, the recorded occupations have to be assigned to the AB, C1, C2, DE classification (or the interviewer's classification checked).

In contrast to the many pitfalls of coding, data entry is a straightforward process. Data from each questionnaire is entered into the computer through the keyboard, with codes punched in one question or column at a time. The data entry programme normally prompts the required input. The work is routine and staff with some experience can build up high work speeds. Since normally only the numeric keyboard is used, typing skill is not necessary.

Data entry.

3. Data validation
Most analysis software includes some data validation routines. If, for example, a response should be a single entry, the validation check will throw up questionnaires where a multi-entry has been wrongly used. Similarly, logic checks will flag problems of data entry incompatible with the questionnaire routing or where there are no responses at all. What this sort of validation will not identify, however, is simple errors, such as punching a code 1 (yes) when the response was actually 2 (no). Such problems can only be minimised by double-entry punching and staff training. The principle of double-entry punching is that after a questionnaire has been entered by one member of staff, another repeats the process and the programme identifies any differences. This will improve overall standards but is, of course, expensive.

Double-entry punching improves the overall standards of the results but is expensive.

4. Hole count
A hole count shows the numbers for each response for each question and, therefore, provides a quick print-out of top-line results – a hole count can be run off as soon as data entry is complete. However, the data from a hole count needs 'decoding' – responses may be shown by column number only, without any question wording or titling. An example of a hole count is shown below in Table 7.11.

As well as providing top-line results, hole counts can be used to identify editing, coding or punching problems – for example, responses to a

Table 7.11 *Analysis of results by hole count (percentages are by row; total sample size 898.)*

Question	Total count	1	2	3	4	5	6	7	8	9	10	11	12	13	14	15	16	17	18	19
													Hole count							
Q1A Catalogues received	770	298	233	235	45	28	21	26	124	46	41	22	15	47	58	0	28	1	0	101
	100.0	38.7	30.3	30.5	5.8	3.6	2.7	3.4	16.1	6.0	5.3	2.9	1.9	6.1	7.5	0.0	3.6	0.1	0.0	13.1
Q1B Catalogues agent for	291	70	53	55	2	1	0	30	1	38	12	43	21	54	12	0	5	0	0	20
	100.0	24.1	18.2	18.9	0.7	0.3	0.0	10.3	0.3	13.1	4.1	14.8	7.2	18.6	4.1	0.0	1.7	0.0	0.0	6.9
Q2A Catalogues bought from 6 mths	898	338	288	264	24	19	14	60	62	71	43	64	44	100	74	0	38	1	35	120
	100.0	37.6	32.1	29.4	2.7	2.1	1.6	6.7	6.9	7.9	4.8	7.1	4.9	11.1	8.2	0.0	4.2	0.1	3.9	13.4
Q3A Sections consider buying from	898	648	383	207	285	415	214	275	265	235	170	34								
	100.0	72.2	42.7	23.1	31.7	46.2	23.8	30.6	29.5	26.2	18.9	3.8								
Q4A Items not currently included	898	732	166																	
	100.0	81.5	18.5																	
Q5A Sections never consider buying	898	27	155	55	47	23	190	41	119	87	123	448								
	100.0	3.0	17.3	6.1	5.2	2.6	21.2	4.6	13.3	9.7	13.7	49.9								
Q6A Finding items of my size	898	56	125	95	296	288	38													
	100.0	6.2	13.9	10.6	33.0	32.1	4.2													
Q6B Finding my particular fitting	898	57	163	106	282	228	62													
	100.0	6.3	18.2	11.8	31.4	25.4	6.9													
Q6C The measurement guide	898	12	42	127	338	278	101													
	100.0	1.3	4.7	14.1	37.6	31.0	11.2													
Q6D Info. regarding monthly stats.	898	19	31	103	240	390	115													
	100.0	2.1	3.5	11.5	26.7	43.4	12.8													

question not adding up to the expected total. As explained later, hole counts are also very useful when specifying the final tables.

5. Table specification

The researcher in charge of the project, or the report writer, has to decide the form or specification of the final table. For each table, decisions have to be made. For example:

- The question to be analysed
- Filtering
- The cross-analysis and cross-breaks (these are often standard for a run of tables)
- Table titling and labelling
- Whether to percentage by row or (more usually) column
- Whether responses are to be ranked in order of magnitude (for example, the most common reason given listed first)
- The inclusion of mean scores or other statistical calculations

Some of these decisions have to be made by the researcher in charge while others can be left to data processing staff. The specifications will also have to be input in a form acceptable to the computer package, which may require some specialist knowledge (quite a lot if the package is not user-friendly).

A common problem in market research is table diarrhoea. Every question is cross-analysed by a dozen or more other questions and the end result is a stack of print-out that nobody can or will use. Not only is this wasteful in time and paper, but it makes the report writing process that much harder. So much rubbish has to be sifted to find the data that is of some use. The problem is best avoided at the specification stage, with perhaps each question cross-analysed by only one or two questions and any further analysis being very selective and decided after examination of the initial run or from the hole count. One principle to follow is that if the total responses to the question are less than 100, then almost *any* cross-analysis is likely to be pointless because the sample sizes for the individual columns will be too small to be statistically significant. Checking the hole count will show the likely sample sizes for each column and allow many tables to be abandoned at the specification stage.

Avoid too much cross-analysis.

6. Table output and checking

Once the table specification is set up, table production is a routine

Table 7.12 B & MR 276 89C Gas wall heater study: gas target market (demographics base: all respondents)

No of persons in household	Area			Age						Type of property					No. in household			
	North	Mid-lands	South	18-24	25-34	35-44	45-54	55-64	65+	Flat	Terrace	Semi-det	Det-ached	Bung-alow	1	2	3 & 4	5+
One	65 27%	41 23%	38 29%	2 5%	11 9%	8 10%	8 12%	15 21%	100 55%	14 28%	88 25%	31 25%	3 33%	7 70%	144 100%	0 -	0 -	0 -
Two	72 30%	71 39%	46 35%	14 36%	33 28%	14 18%	23 35%	37 53%	68 37%	19 38%	120 34%	42 34%	4 44%	1 10%	0 -	189 100%	0 -	0 -
Three or four	84 35%	48 26%	37 28%	20 51%	54 46%	38 49%	28 42%	16 23%	12 7%	15 30%	113 32%	37 30%	1 11%	2 20%	0 -	0 -	169 100%	0 -
Five or more	21 9%	19 10%	10 8%	3 8%	20 17%	18 23%	6 9%	2 3%	0 -	2 4%	34 9%	13 11%	1 11%	0 -	0 -	0 -	0 -	50 100%
Don't know/not stated	0 -	3 2%	0 -	0 -	0 -	0 -	1 2%	0 -	2 1%	0 -	3 1%	0 -	0 -	0 -	0 -	0 -	0 -	0 -
Total	242	182	131	39	118	78	66	70	182	50	358	123	9	10	144	189	169	50

matter; usually, the computer can be left to get on with it. A specimen table is shown in Table 7.12.

The final task is table checking. This involves looking for obvious errors: columns not totalling 100 where they should, cross-break bases not adding to the total base, or mistakes in titling or wording. Problems such as these can usually be put right quickly in further print-outs. Where results just look 'odd', it is worth checking for data processing mistakes before either going to the trouble of back-checking respondents or committing yourself publicly to some self-evident nonsense. Table checking will almost certainly suggest the need for additional tables although, bearing our strictures about over-output in mind, we hope not too many.

CHAPTER 8

PRESENTING DATA

The value in information is what is done with it.

It should always be remembered that information on its own is useless. The value in information is what is done with it. And what is done with information depends on how it has been analysed and presented. To be useful, information needs to be understandable, wholly believable and it should direct the reader towards a course of action. Market researchers who believe that the quality of the product is all that counts, and ignore presentation, do so at their own peril. They risk their many hours of work being confined to a dusty shelf.

The art of personal presentations

If personal presentations fail, it is generally because they have *no* structure or objective. You may have done a good job and know your subject inside out, but if the information is not presented in an orderly fashion with conclusions or recommendations clearly stated, it will be deemed a failure by those who see it.

Almost certainly, the objectives of the research will have been decided before the study began and they will be spelt out in the proposal. Refer back to the proposal and think about what the research was intended to achieve. Clearly, your objective for the presentation should be closely tailored to that of the proposal – but you may decide to take a special slant in the presentation. The presentation is an opportunity to lay emphasis on certain points and to bring the focus on to the key issues.

As an illustration, consider the following brief for a market research survey: 'To research consumers' attitudes to a new chocolate bar and to recommend any changes that could improve its acceptability.' At its best, research should try to lead to a decision. With this in mind, and armed with the results of what people think of the new chocolate bar, you may decide that the objective of the presentation should be: 'To recommend that the new chocolate bar should be launched; that it should be targeted at 10 to 25 year olds, but it should be retested after changing the proposed brand name and the recipe by increasing the caramel content.' Of course, there are many occasions in market research where the correct decision is to recommend *not* launching a product or entering a market.

The objective of the presentation is not straying from that of the research as a whole, rather it is becoming more precise. It will include some general data on what people think but it will end in a sharp focus. It will lead to a course of action. The following list suggests some possible objectives for a presentation:

- To convince the audience that it is a good idea to launch a new product.
- To convince the audience that you should enter a new geographical market.
- To convince the audience that you should withdraw from a market.
- To convince the audience that you should raise/lower prices.
- To convince the audience to adopt a certain advertising/branding strategy.
- To convince the audience that you should expand by acquisition – possibly targeting one or more companies.
- To convince the audience to raise/lower the marketing expenditure for a brand.
- To convince the audience that a new distribution strategy is required.
- To convince the audience that improvements should be made to quality.
- To convince the audience that improvements should be made to the availability of the product.

What is the objective of your presentation?

Sometimes, of course, market researchers are simply asked to find out facts about a market. On these occasions, the real objective of the work may not be known to them; indeed, the management may simply wish to be better informed. The objective of the presentation in such circumstances would be to educate the audience rather than to persuade them to take a course of action.

The presentation is not the time to labour every fact and detail unearthed in the study. This is not necessary and, presumably, it can be referred to in the accompanying written report.

1. Keeping the audience in mind

What will the audience be like?

With an objective in mind, you can now begin to think closely about the three elements that make up the presentation: yourself (the researcher), the audience and the information. The audience dictates everything. When you know more about the audience, you can begin to plan the presentation. Here are some important questions you need to ask about the audience before you begin to plan the presentation:

- Who will be there?
- What will be the functional positions of these people?
- What will be their interests in the findings?
- What will they be expecting to hear?
- How many will there be?
- Will any of the audience be arriving late or leaving early?
- How much time is available to address the audience?

2. Preparing yourself

Making a presentation is a cross between a job interview and a lecture. As in a job interview, it is important to make a mark – to be convincing. At the same time, as in a lecture, there is information to impart and a story to tell. The first few presentations you make will be nerve racking, but once you are adept they will become exhilarating and a highlight of the project.

Nervousness in presentations is the result of physical and mental barriers.

3. Coping with physical barriers

Some of the nerves associated with presentations can best be overcome by working on the physical factors that cause them.

Tension and anxiety

Learn to relax using muscle tensioning and relaxing techniques. Breathe from the diaphragm, not from the chest. Learn to think about the audience as ordinary people and friends, not as exalted gods who are out there to trip you up.

Rehearsal

Rehearse, rehearse and rehearse. Before the presentation, say what you have got to say to an empty room, to your colleagues, your family – anybody or nobody – but get used to saying what you have to say. You will need to spend at least two or three times the time allocated to the presentation in practice sessions.

Speaking

Keep your head up and do *not* mumble. Do *not* speak too fast. Moderate your voice so that it sounds interesting. Practise with a tape recorder and aim to speak at 100 words per minute. Learn to pause, to let the audience catch up and let you catch your breath.

Body movement

It is usually better to stand when giving a presentation. It shows respect for the audience and gives you the advantage of some presence. Be careful that you do not have any annoying fidgets that distract the audience. No jangling of money or keys in the pocket; no pacing up and down like a caged animal.

Eye contact

Look at the audience – the whole audience and not just one person. Eye contact communicates honesty, integrity and confidence.

4. Coping with mental barriers

As with physical barriers, there are techniques for coping with the mental pressures associated with presentations.

Think positively

Many researchers are junior executives, much younger than the managers to whom they are presenting. There is a tendency to think, 'Who am I to tell them?' Think positively. You have the knowledge.

Pre-planning

Know your stuff. Go through your work again and again so that you are totally familiar with it. As you rehearse what you are going to say, you will grow in confidence. Adopt a positive attitude and think about all the things you do know, rather than the many things you don't know –

and it is too late to find out. Think about the questions you may be asked. Try to prepare for them. Do not pretend to have knowledge you do not have or you will be sure to be caught out. It is to be expected that you will not know everything, and, as ever, honesty is the best policy.

Answering questions
Try to encourage questions. Audiences like to participate in the presentation. Give careful thought to every question – do not give ill-considered replies. Do not try to score points or put the audience down. Use words like: 'That is an interesting question . . .'

Appearance
A high level of confidence and a positive attitude are helped by dressing for the occasion. Choose clothes that are comfortable and smart. Check your hair. Feel easy about your personal appearance.

Support with visual aids
Visual aids help the audience by clarifying points and adding variety to the presentation. They help you by providing a structure. However, remember that they are there to support the presentation and they should not dominate it.

Pace and length
You may have intended that the presentation should take half an hour but be prepared to be flexible. Watch for signals of boredom or irritation. If necessary, speed up the pace or ditch some of the information you were going to present. You will seldom be criticised for making the presentation too short!

5. The importance of structure

Presentations need structure.

We have seen the importance of structure in all manner of market research activities. It plays its part in briefings, questionnaire design, desk research and it is essential in presentations. By structure, we mean the arrangement and organisation of the information. Without structure, presentations ramble on and are messy.

In its simplest form, the structure of any presentation can be reduced to the following – a beginning, a middle and an end.

Introduction
At the start, you must tell the audience what they can expect to hear and

how long it will take. You should remind them about the objectives of the survey and the methods that were employed. In a 30-minute presentation, the introduction should take no more than five minutes, as people are eagerly waiting to hear the next bit – what you have found out.

What you have found out
The centre piece of the presentation is what you have found out. These are the findings of the survey and they should flow logically and smoothly towards the conclusions. Do not labour the findings. In a 30-minute presentation, they should take 15 minutes.

The conclusions you have arrived at and the recommendations you wish to make
The final 10 minutes of a 30-minute presentation should be given to the drawing of conclusions and the submission of recommendations. In a well-presented study, the conclusions and recommendations will be no surprise. The audience will have arrived there simply by following the logic of what you have been saying.

6. Making use of resources

Presentations must make an impact – and the right sort of impact. You do not want to be remembered as someone who droned on for two hours. Short, snappy presentations are the best. Where possible, you should be 'bold', even provocative. This will keep the audience interested, stir them and make them more likely to remember what has been said and take action.

Unfortunately, we are not all charismatic and gifted presenters. Impact has to be achieved, therefore, by whatever means we can muster. Smart dress and a good structure to the presentation will certainly help, but an extra lift may be required. Audiences become bored after just five minutes of speech. They need a change of pace and texture to keep them interested. Visual aids and prompts become important in breaking the presentation into digestible chunks.

Visual aids are important in presentations.

Table 8.1 lists a number of presentation aids that can be used by the researcher to stimulate and maintain the interest of the audience. A word of caution! There is a danger of 'going over the top' with the aids. Their misuse could result in the presentation appearing gimmicky and they may become a distraction from the real message.

189

Table 8.1 *Advantages and disadvantages of presentation aids*

Presentation aid	Advantages	Disadvantages
Overheads/acetates	Simple and quick to organise; (on most photocopiers) relatively inexpensive to produce; easy to use; can be used in 'daylight'; the presenter is not 'blacked' out; it is easy to alter the sequence or skip slides.	They can be dull; they can be distracting as they are being changed.
35 mm transparencies	Impressive; use can be made of colour and sophisticated graphics; product and location shots can be mixed in; the fixed sequence means a 'slick' presentation.	Takes time to organise; expensive; needs specialised equipment to produce and to project; the room needs to be blacked out; difficult to skip slides; inflexible once you have started.
Flip charts	Simple to use; inexpensive, readily available; flexible.	Needs artistic skills to be impressive; it is time consuming and distracting to prepare during the presentation; no good for complex tables or long quotes.
Product displays	Attention grabbing; generally easy to organise; very meaningful to the audience.	Can be a distraction; not possible to organise with large or expensive products.

In selecting the visual aid, it is important to consider the type of room in which the presentation will be made. If the presentation is to be made to just one person in a small room, it would be wrong to use any aids at all. In these circumstances, it is best to sit down and talk through the findings in an informal way. The advantages and disadvantages of different types of presentation aids are listed in Table 8.1.

Presenting quantitative information

1. The use of tables

Quantitative data can be as dry as dust. However, resist the temptation to make an acetate of all the tables in the report and use these for the presentation. This is sure to put the audience to sleep. Only use tables where it is necessary to refer to the *actual* figures. Thus, it may be appropriate to present a table of a company's balance sheet or a table showing the exchange rate of currencies. In these cases, the audience is interested in the *precise* figures, which are displayed. In most other circumstances, the quantitative data should be converted into a chart or diagram.

Use tables to show precise figures only.

Consider the information in Table 8.2 which was contained in a draft report. How many things can you see wrong with the table?

Table 8.2 *Dissatisfaction with motor, personal accident or sickness and holiday insurance*

	motor	pers. acc./ sick	holiday
unweighted bases; those dissatisfied	149	28	33
cause of dissatisfaction	%	%	%
misled by broker/salesman into taking unnecessary/expensive policy	1.2	16.3	–
special conditions imposed (inc. excess)	6.45	7.0	6.6
cost of policy/premium increase	39.3	27.4	11.4
claim not covered by policy	1.6	9.9	15.2
claim not met in full	6.7	17.4	17.1
long delay in dealing with claim	19.8	19.1	29.0
other complaints	26.9	12.6	10.2
not stated	6.1	10.8	24.4

If we consider the purpose of a table, we can begin to see what the faults are with this submission. A table is a series of data. And a good table is one that quickly and clearly communicates patterns of information to the reader. If we look back to our example table, the first thing that it should shout at the audience is *what* the table is all about. In other words, the *title* should say what to expect. The title on our table could be improved, perhaps saying more simply: 'Reasons why policy holders are dissatisfied with their insurance policies.' The fact that different types of insurance are covered is self-evident when the table is examined.

The column headings are the next thing we see. These need to be shortened so they are understandable without being too cumbersome at the head of the column. In our example, we can see that the heading 'pers.acc./sick' is fighting for room with its shorter neighbours and the attempts to summarise the three words have resulted in some peculiarities. A simple statement 'accident/sickness' would be better. It is also worth making the headings stand out by emboldening or underlining.

The first row is likely to cause trouble for most readers. It provides some figures alongside the statement 'unweighted bases; those dissatisfied'. This table was included as part of a report aimed at high street insurance brokers and they are unlikely to have any idea what unweighted bases are. In fact, they refer to the number of people that were interviewed; it would have been far better to have simply said 'sample size'. It would also have been better to position the row at the bottom of the table, since readers expect to see data in the first row corresponding to the column headings.

Moving down the table, we are presented with a line that includes, on the left-hand side, a heading and a '%' sign above each column. It would be better if this line was incorporated into a simple grouping which presents all the column headings together.

A point in favour of this table is that it does not contain too much data. A common mistake of researchers is to include columns of percentages *and* the absolute numbers, when the percentages alone would suffice. However, the table contains two further errors commonly found in data presentation. First, the accuracy of the figures to one and two decimal points is superfluous and confusing. A good table enables the reader to relate one set of figures to another and so pick out a pattern. This is made difficult when there are lots of figures to contend with. The mind finds it much easier to assimilate and remember figures that are limited to just two whole digits. There is, therefore, a strong argument for *rounding* all figures in tables to two whole digits. Of course, the rule cannot always be applied. If the data is required for precision, or for subsequent analysis, the full figure must be given. (Currency changes, weighting factors, chemical constituents, and so on, should all be given in full rather than rounded figures.)

Where possible, round all figures equally, so they are easily compared.

Returning to the data in the table, we can see that a problem is caused by the rows being presented in no particular order. Again, remembering that a good table allows the reader to relate figures to each other, it would be greatly improved if the rows were ordered. Positioning the most important row at the top of the table would give the reader an obvious benchmark by which to compare all the other responses. Presenting the list in declining rank order immediately highlights that 'policy costs/increases' are the most important causes of dissatisfaction for all types of policy. Second in importance, and a long way behind, is the dissatisfaction caused by delays in processing the claims. In a table such as the one we are examining, it is not easy to choose the column that dictates the order of the rows because there are a number of columns – there is no total or average column that can guide us. We must, therefore, make judgements and rank the rows in the order of importance as they seem to us. Thus, although 16 per cent of people with a personal accident/sickness insurance expressed dissatisfaction because they were misled into a needlessly expensive policy, this problem did not arise with motor or holiday insurance. Overall, it appears to be a less important reason for dissatisfaction than 'the claim not being covered by the policy' and can, therefore, take a more lowly position in the table. (It is worth mentioning at this point that most tables are improved by having a 'total' column, which presents the overall picture against which all the other columns can be compared.)

Order the rows by rank.

Provide a reference point for comparing data.

The rules of ordering data according to the size of response must not be applied to all tables. For example, if the table showed a scalar response, then the data would follow the scale. For example, if figures were being presented on people's satisfaction with a product on a five-point scale, then 'very satisfied' would always take the top slot while 'not satisfied at all' would be at the bottom – irrespective of how many responses there were to the different answers.

In reorganising the table on dissatisfaction with insurance policies, we

193

face the problem of deciding what to do with the 'dustbin categories' such as 'other complaints' and 'not stated'. Commonsense must be the arbiter. In most tables, these categories fit comfortably at the bottom. They are, after all, a different type of response, providing extra information on groups of respondents who have no opinion or some oddball view, which in isolation is unimportant, although taken together amounts to quite a lump.

A little bit of cleaning up of the words used to describe the reasons for dissatisfaction and the revised table is nearly finished (Table 8.3). However, having reordered the rows, we can easily see that the sum of the columns exceeds 100 per cent. This is because a policy holder can be dissatisfied for more than one reason. It is a 'multi-response question' and this should be made clear in the table. Tables should state along the bottom what a column adds up to or, in the case of a multi-response question, explain why it does not add up to 100 per cent.

Finally, the table should show where the data has come from and the date to which it refers. Without this information, the reader finds it difficult to judge the accuracy of the data.

Table 8.3 *Reasons why policy holders are dissatisfied with their insurance policies*

Cause of dissatisfaction	Type of policy		
	Motor	Accident/ sickness	Holiday
	%	%	%
Cost of policy/premium increase	39	27	11
Delay in dealing with claim	20	19	29
Claim not met in full	7	17	17
Claim not covered by policy	2	10	15
Special conditions imposed	6	7	7
Misled into expensive policy	1	16	–
Other complaints	27	13	10
Not stated	6	11	24
Total	*	*	*
Sample size	149	28	33

* Multi-response and therefore total exceeds 100 per cent.
Source: *The Insurance Handbook*, 1987.

This exercise highlights the following golden rules for presenting statistical data in tables:

- Use clear, meaningful and concise headings and labels. Highlight them with underlining, bold or special typefaces.
- Keep the data simple and don't overcrowd the table.
- Wherever possible, round the data to just two whole figures.
- Order the rows in declining rank unless dealing with scalar data.
- Look for opportunities to present 'total' or 'average' columns or rows which give reference points for comparing other data.
- Show the source of the data.

2. The use of charts and diagrams

A picture has always been worth a thousand words and a graph is only a variation on the pictorial theme. Diagrams can simplify and communicate more quickly figures than words or tables. In the past, diagrams have had to be drawn by hand, which takes time and thought to create. Today, with inexpensive graphics software coupled to a personal computer and a plotter, graphics can easily be prepared – indeed, they are becoming expected in executive reports and presentations.

Like tables, diagrams are also a means of analysing and presenting data. However, diagrams are powerful because they give *instant* impact. They can be used as a personal aid in analysing data, they can clarify a point in a written report or they can be made into a slide for a presentation. The use of a diagram affects its design. A diagram designed for your own purposes to help you understand a point could be far more complex than one shown on a screen in a presentation. Our interest here is with charts that are used as a communication device – to deliver data off the page or off the screen. To be effective, these must be simple.

Let us assume that a decision has been made to use diagrams to present data in a report. The information is currently available in tables and we need to convert this to an appropriate chart. The first task is to decide on the type of chart to be used. Very simply, there are five major types:

- Pie diagrams
- Graphs
- Bar charts
- Charts comparing two variables
- Organisational type charts

195

The choice between these most common types of diagram is not always clear. The following guidelines suggest where they are best suited.

Pie diagrams

Pie diagrams are useful for showing spatial differences.

Pie diagrams, as the name suggests, present the data in circles with slices marked out to show the size of segments. They are used when it is necessary to show parts of a whole. One of the most frequent examples we come across in marketing is the use of the pie diagram to illustrate the breakdown of a market into its segments or to show the shares of the companies that supply it (see Figure 8.1). If you need to provide an assessment of market shares, but in truth cannot be sure of the precise figures for each company, then a pie diagram is useful, as it takes the emphasis off the spurious precision of a table and puts it on to the *spatial* differences between the companies – which is usually the most important issue.

Graphs

Graphs can be used to highlight trends over time.

Graphs are used to analyse trends over time (see Figure 8.2). They are used instead of bar charts (which can perform the same purpose) when there are many data points – say more than 20. Graphs give a smoother line to a time series that covers many years. The eye can pick out the trend in the data and project it forward, so obtaining a feel for the future.

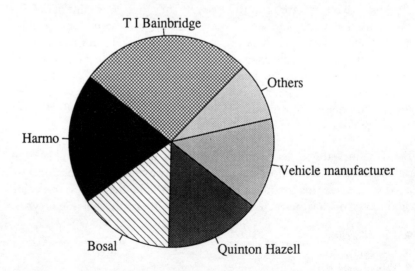

Figure 8.1 *Shares in the replacement car exhaust market (1986)*
Source: Business & Market Research plc.

Market size (£ million retail prices)

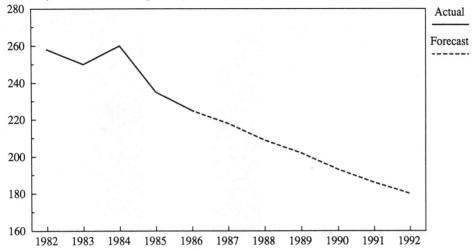

Figure 8.2 *Trends in the UK replacement exhaust market (1982–86 = actual; 1987–92 = forecast)*
Source: Business & Market Research plc.

You can have more than one line on a graph but be careful; it can become very confusing if the lines are close together and keep criss-crossing over.

Bar charts
There are a number of different types of bar chart. At its simplest, it consists of a single bar broken down to show its component parts, very much like a pie diagram (see Figure 8.3).

In a horizontal form, bar charts can be used to show the range of responses to a particular question or the number of firms that fulfil certain criteria (see Figure 8.4).

Bar charts have an important advantage over line graphs in that they can show both a trend *and* movements within segments; and since an important part of marketing is about *recognising* segments, this could explain the popularity of the bar chart for presenting data. Splitting up each column shows the trend while lining up the columns next to each other shows how both the whole and the component parts of a market have moved over time (see Figure 8.5).

Bar charts can show both a trend and movements within a segment.

197

Percentage retail exhaust sales

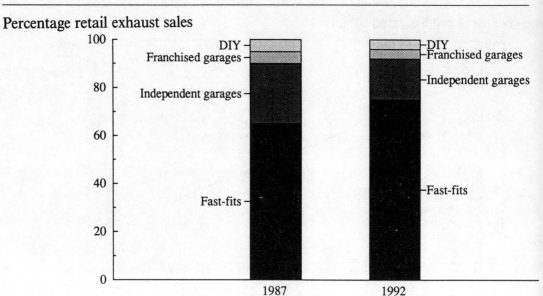

Figure 8.3   *The future growth of fast-fits (1987 to 1992)*
Source: Business & Market Research plc.

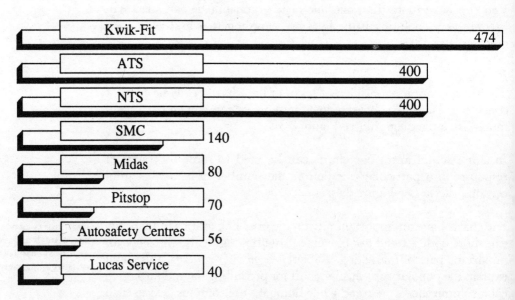

Figure 8.4   *Major fast-fit exhaust centres (number of outlets in mid-1987)*
Source: Business & Market Research plc.

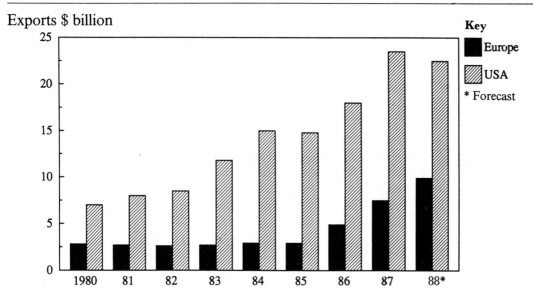

Figure 8.5   *Trends in Taiwanese exports to Europe and USA*
Source: Business & Market Research plc.

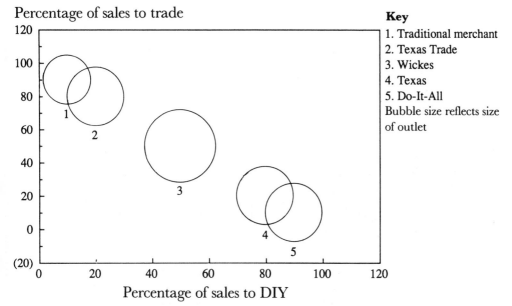

Figure 8.6   *The positioning of builders merchants*
Source: Business & Market Research plc.

199

Charts comparing two variables

In marketing, we often need to position companies or see the relationship between two variables. For this, we need a diagram, with the usual x and y axis, on which we can position companies according to the type of business they have or the relationship between (say) price and demand (see Figure 8.6).

Organisational type charts

Organisational charts show the flow of data. The most familiar is, perhaps, the management organisation chart, but the same pictorial presentation could equally be used to show the flow of work in a market research project.

The labelling of charts needs more care and attention than tables. Charts need a title, which should say simply and clearly what is being portrayed. Scales should be marked and there must be a key or legend that tells the reader what is what. Wherever possible, key words should be positioned horizontally, otherwise they are difficult to read. This can sometimes be difficult but words that follow the bicycle spokes of a pie diagram require you to crick your neck to see what they say.

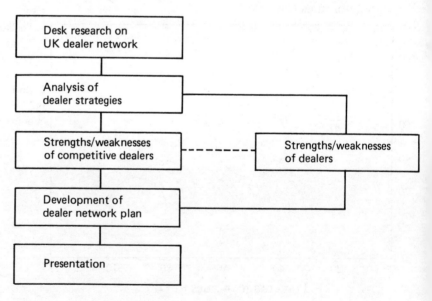

Figure 8.7 *Dealer development study*
Source: Business & Market Research plc.

When diagrams appear not to work in their conversion from table to picture, it is most probably due to the fact that they have become over-complicated, with too much shading, too many lines and too much information. Charts that are prepared as one-offs for a presentation can be prepared on a plotter and full use can be made of colour. However, if they are going to be reproduced as part of a photocopied report, it is wise to design the shading of the chart with this in mind. The important rule when designing a diagram is to keep everything out that you possibly can. This may mean splitting up a table so that it becomes two or three diagrams.

Beware of making diagrams over-complicated, since they will lose their impact.

Presenting qualitative information

Qualitative information in a market research project is the opinion and anecdotal comment that has been unearthed and which makes up the findings. In presenting qualitative research, it is important that the story unfolds as the case is being made or a point described. For this reason, qualitative findings can be harder to present than quantitative findings, as there may not be any firm facts. In group discussion work, the researcher must avoid the temptation to convert a collection of views into a hard and fast figure. The number of respondents attending the groups is so small that results would be different if measured on a large scale. To give a proportion is to risk it becoming accepted as 'holy writ', when it is only a very rough estimate, probably not even based on a head count.

Qualitative research findings are in special need of a firm structure. Without structure, the presentation will ramble on. Headings and flagging statements are needed so that the audience can quickly understand the context of any comments.

Because qualitative findings are based on respondents' opinions, albeit interpreted by the researcher, it can be useful to display some of the comment as direct speech, for example: 'I have bought their bread for years. However, I just can't get used to their thicker slices so I have changed to Sunwheat.' The use of quotes in reports and presentations makes it plain to the audience that the comment is not emanating from the researcher. This gives it greater impact. Furthermore, direct speech is generally found to be more interesting by the audience and it will enliven a presentation.

201

Presentations on industrial markets are usually based on qualitative information, even if much of the information is quantitative – market sizes, market shares, etc. For example, unstructured interviews may have been carried out with a number of people to obtain their views on the market size for a product. The researcher will weigh up the accuracy of the various respondents and arrive at a best estimate, which is presented as a quantity – 'The market is worth five million units per year valued at £10 million at retail prices.' The audience requires some feel for the accuracy of this figure. Although it may be an estimate based on the judgement of the researcher, an explanation is needed to show how the final figure was determined.

Often, qualitative concepts and findings can be converted to charts or diagrams. These can be as simple or as complicated as the researcher chooses and may vary from those prepared on computer graphics packages through to a felt tip pen scribbled on to a flipchart to emphasise a point in a verbal debrief.

Writing effective market research reports

Information should be communicated as clearly and easily as possible.

Nearly all market research projects end up in written report form. A written report is required as a reference document so that anybody can read the findings at some time in the future. And, since the reader may not be fully *au fait* with the background to the project, the report should be comprehensive. It needs a full and clear explanation of what was undertaken, how it was carried out, what was found and what conclusions were reached.

We are not suggesting that market researchers should adopt one rigid report writing style. This would be too restricting and it would stifle the flair and distinction that sets good work apart. However, there are a number of guidelines that the market researcher is advised to heed when writing reports. Three factors, in particular, should be borne in mind before putting pen to paper:

- Your aim is to communicate information as clearly as possible to the reader.
- Assume that the reader is a busy person who wants to understand your report on the first reading.
- Assume that the reader has paid good money to carry out the research and it is only courteous to ensure that the report is thoroughly checked and spelt correctly.

1. Report structure and content

The structure of a report enables the reader to find his way around quickly. A good structure and attractive layout presents a good image. The content of the report is the 'meat' in which the reader is interested.

To achieve a suitable structure, prepare a rough plan before writing anything. This may be a simple draft of the chapters and section headings. You can even go further by writing down the main points to be covered under each section or, in the case of reports written from structured questionnaires, build a list of the tables that will be included in each section of the report.

When you are planning the report, always read the proposal first. After all, the proposal is what was agreed at the outset and it is the 'contract' against which the work has been carried out. Just because you have found out a lot of peripheral information, this does not mean that it should all be included in the report.

Always refer back to the proposal.

Here are some rules that you should bear in mind when writing clear, effective reports:

- *Keep the report short.* Make a point briefly, clearly and just once. This does not mean that 100-page reports are always inappropriate, but wherever possible reports should be much shorter than this. Remember your busy client!
- *Be consistent.* Be consistent with spellings, headings, typefaces, etc. Also, be consistent with your facts. Don't talk about a market size of £5 million on one page and then, without explanation, include a table that contradicts this.
- *Go from the general to the particular.* When you are commenting on tables or writing about group discussions, start by talking about what most people said and then move on to specific comments.
- *Have a logical structure.* As always, structure is the key. The report should have an introduction, a middle and an end.
- *Keep the report in balance.* Ensure that the correct amount of weight and emphasis is given to all the subjects covered in the report. Just because you know a lot about something in particular, it is not an excuse to wax lyrical.
- *Always label tables and diagrams.* Make sure that the label to the table or diagram says what it is. Wherever appropriate, the source and sample size should be given.

- *When commenting on tables, put the text first.* The commentary should precede the table and should confine itself to data contained in the table.
- *Know your facts.* Nothing should be put in a report that you don't understand yourself or could not explain if asked.
- *State the source of key facts.* If there is a statement in the report about market size or the performance of a company, the reader has the right to know if it is your opinion or that of some expert you are quoting.
- *Read and check your report.* Do not rely on word-processing spell checkers or on other people's typing – checking a report is your responsibility.

2. Grammar and good English

Where there is a short word, use it. Do not use jargon in the report unless it really cannot be avoided. If the reader has to look up a word in the dictionary, you are not showing how clever you are; rather, you are displaying a lack of sympathy for the audience.

As a general rule, sentences should be constructed with a subject, verb and object, as in 'The cat (subject) sat (verb) on the mat (object).' It is much clearer and better English to say 'Half of the respondents we interviewed would be likely to purchase an independently tested product' than 'An independently tested product would be likely to be purchased by one-half of the respondents interviewed.'

Again, as a general rule, sentences should be short rather than long. When a sentence exceeds 25 words, it may be worth splitting it into two or making it more manageable by means of 'bullet points'. Bullet points have the advantage of:

- Letting the reader see immediately how many points you are trying to make
- Relieving the boredom of long, dense text
- Making each point simple and easy to understand

As with all devices, when used too much, they can make the report stilted. However, it is better to aim at a concise report than one which is a literary work with long convoluted sentences.

A common mistake made by market researchers is to refer to companies in the plural. A company is an 'it' and not a 'they'. You should talk about 'Smith Limited and its plans' and not 'their plans'.

Punctuation

Punctuation in a sentence exists to make its construction perfectly clear. Here are some guidelines on the use of punctuation, which will lead to improved clarity in reports:

- *Commas.* Commas are used to break sentences and are inserted at the point where, if you were to read the text out loud, you would pause.
- *Brackets.* The contents of the brackets have no bearing on the main sentence; they could be omitted and the sentence would still make sense. They are used for after-thoughts, brief explanations or references.
- *Colons and semi-colons.* Colons are used mainly to separate a clause that introduces a list, quotation, summary, etc. The semi-colon provides a slightly heavier pause than a comma but not as heavy as a full-stop. It is useful for separating two sentences that could stand alone, but are closely connected in sense.
- *Capitals.* Capital letters should be used for proper names – names of people, names of places, brand names, etc. If you have your own predilections for using capital letters, at least be consistent.
- *The apostrophe.* This simple little mark has two main functions: to denote that you have left out one or more letters in a word, and to denote possession. 'It's' is short for 'it is' or 'it has'. 'Don't' is short for 'do not'.

Five rules to remember about punctuation.

◄ CHAPTER 9 ►

COMMISSIONING MARKET RESEARCH

The preceding chapters of this book have described how to do market research. This chapter discusses how to get others to do the work. For convenience, we will refer to those commissioned to carry out market research on your behalf as an agency or market research agency. For the purposes of discussion, we assume in this chapter that a fairly large project may be involved. However, many of the points also apply to smaller projects, although some of the steps might be short-circuited.

The contents of this chapter apply to all types of market research – the process of choosing an agency to carry out consumer research is the same as for business-to-business research.

Why use an outside agency?

It is worth being clear in your own mind why an outside agency is being considered in situations where an in-house researcher could undertake the work. Table 9.1 will help you to decide if you really do need outside help. Of course, the importance of the factors may change in different projects.

Decide if an outside agency is needed to do the research.

Lack of time and a shortage of staff are self-evident reasons for using an agency. In the same way, problems of geographical coverage may cause you to seek outside help. Whatever your competence as a market researcher, there will always be times when you need to buy in skills that are lacking internally. No one is capable of carrying out all types of

Table 9.1 *Reasons for using an outside agency to carry out research*

Reason	Importance		
	Major	**Secondary**	**Little/none**
Timetable too short	[ ]	[ ]	[ ]
Lack of staff	[ ]	[ ]	[ ]
Geographical coverage too large	[ ]	[ ]	[ ]
Lack of in-house expertise	[ ]	[ ]	[ ]
Research must be anonymous	[ ]	[ ]	[ ]
Research needs to be objective/impartial	[ ]	[ ]	[ ]
In-company politics	[ ]	[ ]	[ ]

When deciding to use an outside agency, weigh up the pros and cons.

research equally well. Also, there are some general skills such as proficiency in a language that may be an essential requirement in some studies.

The four reasons discussed so far for using an agency relate to a lack of resources in-house. The other reasons are concerned with the nature of the situation in which the work is being carried out.

Commercially, it may be essential for the identity of the organisation commissioning the work to remain confidential. This could be the case when the research is linked to the possible acquisition of another company, or where you are thinking of entering a different market or launching a new product. Particularly in business-to-business markets, where there are a limited number of players, competitors may infer your strategy merely because you are carrying out research. However, such considerations can reach paranoid dimensions. More often than not, a competitor is unlikely to be able to react, even if it is known that your company is interested in a particular area. There is so much other data he is lacking.

It hardly needs mentioning, but all researchers should be objective in

Agencies can be totally objective.

their work. Sometimes, however, it can be hard, especially if, as an in-house researcher, you have been closely involved in a venture that must now be subjected to cold scrutiny. A good agency can be totally objective, as it does not have any emotional links with the project. Its fees are met even if the results are negative. The agency's concern is to predict accurately whether the proposed venture will succeed or fail without being influenced by conventional wisdom or the strongly held views of the managers involved in the commissioning company.

Not only should research be objective, it should be seen to be so, and this leads to the issue of in-house politics. Sometimes it is just better for outsiders to carry out and report the research, particularly if the issue being researched has split the management team into factions.

Selecting an agency

The process of selecting an agency can be summarised as follows:

1. Prepare brief
2. Agree brief internally
3. Set criteria for agency selection
4. Draw up list of possible agencies
5. Contact agencies to establish interest and broad experience
6. Prepare shortlist of agencies to tender
7. Brief shortlisted agencies
8. Evaluate proposals
9. Make final choice

Of course, not all of these steps are always necessary. For example, if only one person is involved in the issues underlying the brief, then steps 1 and 2 can be combined. Similarly, when you have commissioned market research projects regularly, you develop a relationship with agencies and a knowledge of their capabilities. Therefore, there may be no need for steps 4 and 5.

1. The brief

The brief should state what is expected of the research.

It is desirable to prepare a formal written brief, stating what is expected of the research, before holding any meetings with agencies or even contacting them. Preparing the brief will clarify your mind as well as telling the agency what you expect from them.

The market for industrial plugs and sockets
John Smith, Marketing Manager
May 1989

Introduction

Our company is well established as a supplier of domestic plugs and sockets, and our market share is around 15 per cent. It has been suggested that we now enter the market for industrial plugs and sockets. These products are high in value (compared to domestic) and the market may be less price sensitive. We have very little knowledge about the market and, therefore, need to consider research to guide a market entry decision and plan a strategy. If we enter the market, a 'copy cat' product range is envisaged.

Objective of the research

To provide marketing data on industrial plugs and sockets to guide an entry decision and strategy.

Geographic coverage

Great Britain (UK but not Northern Ireland).

Information coverage

The following areas are considered important but suggestions for other areas to include would be welcome.

(1) Market size in value/volume.
(2) Major product groupings within the market and a breakdown of the market by these groups.
(3) Trends in the size of the market; last 3–5 years and predictions for a similar period forward.
(4) The existing manufacturers or other major suppliers, with brief profiles, including their position in the market and their marketing approaches.
(5) Types of distributor involved in the market, their attitudes to the products and suppliers, and their possible interest in additional sources of supply.
(6) Typical end-users of industrial plugs and sockets, segmentation of the market by major groupings of users, how they buy the products (importance of price, design, quality, etc.) and indications of their satisfaction with current ranges.

Research methods

Agencies are encouraged to suggest in their proposals a suitable research method. However, it is likely that some interviewing will be necessary with users, distributors and possibly manufacturing suppliers. Some desk research is likely to be necessary, to provide a background. Agencies should state the number and type of interviews that will be carried out with each group of respondent. The number of consultant days allocated to each activity within the study should be provided in the proposal.

It is envisaged that the agency carrying out the work will prepare and present a report, which should include both factual data and interpretation/conclusions.

Timing

Provisionally, we anticipate:

- Briefing of agencies by May 22
- Selection of agency by May 31
- Completion by July 28

Budget

A fairly modest level of investment is envisaged if we enter the market. A maximum research budget of around £15,000 should be realistic and appropriate. The costings should separate out the fee and expenses.

Figure 9.1   *Specimen brief*

Figure 9.1 presents a specimen brief to illustrate the points that should be covered. The brief starts with an indication of why the research is being considered. Every project should have a clear objective and some of the principles involved in setting these were discussed in Chapter 1. The geographic coverage may be worth stating for the benefit of tendering agencies. Where the research is to be multi-national, the countries should be spelt out. To say 'Europe' is too vague. The brief should also list the main areas of information you expect to be covered.

With some knowledge of market research methods, you will almost certainly have a view on how the work should be carried out. It may be worth including your suggestion in the brief and asking the agency for alternatives. Giving the agency a guide to your thinking could be helpful, as the agency could spend time and effort proposing a large quantitative programme when you feel committed to a qualitative approach. The fact that the two methods are not the same will require one or other of you to debate the limitations of each and eventually agree on the optimum approach. In any case, it is nearly always best to give the agency scope to suggest the methods they believe are appropriate. After all, as consultants, they should be able to recommend a technically good approach.

Give the agency scope to show their professionalism.

A timetable for the completion of the research should be stated in the brief. This should be realistic and take into account the time involved in choosing an agency, as well as actually doing the work. At the time of writing the brief, the timetable is almost bound to be loose and dates for the stages in the research programme will help you to make realistic changes in the schedule.

If you have had very little experience in commissioning research, you will find that setting a budget is difficult. You may have no idea of the scale of charges. However, you should have some broad indication of how much the research data is 'worth' to your company, especially in relation to the level of expenditure linked to the decisions that the research is guiding. Research to support an investment of £1 million may justify a larger budget than if the capital expenditure is considerably less. Also, the amount that can be spent on the research may be constrained by what has been allowed for in your internal budget. Sometimes special provision has to be made for a project if there is no money available in the budget.

If a budget does exist for the project, it need not necessarily be revealed to the tendering agencies. However, in fairness to the agencies, they will need to know either the research method being considered or an approximation of the available budget. Without these parameters, the agencies could spend much time and effort designing research programmes that are rejected as far too sophisticated and expensive.

2. The selection criteria
Having briefed the agencies, you must have some criteria for selecting one of them to carry out the work. Some relevant criteria are suggested in Table 9.2. However, the importance of the criteria will vary, according to the project.

Other things being equal, an agency that has carried out good work for you in the past may be preferred. However, some experimentation is to be encouraged.

Table 9.2 *Criteria for agency selection*

Criteria	Importance		
	Very important	**Some importance**	**Little/no importance**
Past experience of agency	[ ]	[ ]	[ ]
Product area experience	[ ]	[ ]	[ ]
Market experience	[ ]	[ ]	[ ]
Have relevant data available	[ ]	[ ]	[ ]
Experience of proposed research techniques	[ ]	[ ]	[ ]
Experience of interpretation and drawing conclusions	[ ]	[ ]	[ ]
Skills and qualifications of the project team	[ ]	[ ]	[ ]

Use this checklist when screening a market research company.

While experience of products is often thought to be important, an understanding of how different types of market work may be more critical. Furthermore, experience in your market can prove beneficial as data relevant to the project may be readily available, thereby saving time and costs. However, beware. It is not unknown for tendering agencies to embroider their claims. Also, where the information sought is attitudinal, it is unlikely that any relevant data will be freely available (as agencies are not at liberty to use work carried out for some other client). There is also an argument for choosing researchers without preconceptions.

Decide at the outset what type of service you require.

You should decide at the outset what type of service you expect from the agency. The agency will be able to provide a menu of services. They could, for example, supply you just with completed questionnaires (known as 'interview-only' work). On the other hand, they could provide tabulated responses to questions, or a full service of interviewing plus interpretation and conclusions relevant to your future actions. If

212

you require the latter service, it would be advisable to seek some indication of the agency's capabilities in this respect.

Obviously, it is important that the agency uses qualified and experienced personnel throughout all stages of the work. Depending on the type of study, it may be important to meet and vet the key executives who will be involved. This is particularly applicable in qualitative research or where the final author of the report is going to draw marketing conclusions.

3. Contacting agencies

For a large project, you should seek proposals from about three agencies. Proposal preparation not only requires agencies to put in considerable work, but you must also spend time briefing and evaluating. To ask for more than about three proposals, therefore, not only wastes the time of several agencies (at best, each only has a 33 per cent chance of winning) but your own as well. Before inviting three agencies to propose formally, you may need to contact quite a few more to identify those who are most likely to be able to carry out the project well. No two agencies are alike; each has unique experience, a style of working and, above all, different people. None is 'the best', but some are better at particular types of work.

An initial shortlist of suitable agencies can be drawn up from personal experience and mail shots received from agencies or directories. In the UK, there are three specialist sources, each of which lists market research agencies together with their specialisations and size:

- *The Association of British Market Research Companies Handbook*
- *Market Research Society Yearbook*
- *Industrial Marketing Research Association Directory*

The details in these directories are provided by the agencies themselves and, therefore, include some puffery. However, for any particular requirement, most will clearly be unsuitable because their specialisation lies in other areas, so it should not be hard to list six to ten agencies that appear suited to your own project.

The agencies on this initial shortlist can then be contacted by telephone or standard letter. The research requirement should be briefly outlined and the agency asked to indicate their interest in carrying out the work, whether they can meet the timetable and, broadly, their relevant expertise. It should be made clear that only a brief response is required initially.

Select about three agencies from your initial shortlist.

On the basis of the responses from the agencies contacted, the initial shortlist can be pruned to the three you would like to prepare proposals. Generally, agencies make no charge for the considerable time they put into initial meetings and proposal writing, and, in fairness, you should only put agencies to this trouble if:

- You are prepared to give equal consideration to each agency's proposals.
- You are committed in principle to going ahead with the research.
- You have a budget available to pay for the work.

4. Briefing agencies

A meeting is imperative.

The selected agencies should be sent copies of your full brief. You should also, however, expect to meet them and discuss in some detail both the background to the research and your requirements. Even if you do not suggest a meeting, they should.

The briefing meeting can be at your own office; the agency might wish to visit you as part of the process of understanding your company and its needs. However, if at all possible, visit the agency's premises as well. Seeing the researchers on their own ground will give you a far better and more candid picture of their operation.

The briefing meeting itself is a two-way process; the agency needs to understand your requirements and you need to learn about the agency. On the whole, you can be passive and let the researcher ask you questions to establish your needs. You will by now have given the agency your written briefing and the researcher should have questions to ask. If the agency has no questions, you can reasonably doubt the agency's skills as researchers – researchers should be questioners. However, bear in mind that the agency at this stage only needs to know enough to prepare thorough proposals and, until it is commissioned, some areas of information about your own operation may be unnecessary. Indeed, you may wish to hold back some confidential data until an agency is selected; this will be understood.

Make it clear that you expect the agency to prepare full written proposals. The agency will almost certainly indicate its own relevant skills and experience in preparing written proposals. At the briefing meeting, however, you should establish some background information which may influence your decision on which agency to commission.

Some judgement about the size of the agency in relation to the project is important. Very small agencies can carry out work to the highest standards, but problems will arise if the project is larger than they can handle with their available resources, especially bearing in mind that other work will almost certainly be in hand. Be wary if the value of the work proposed is more than 10 per cent of the agency's annual turnover.

The key in any project is the quality of the staff involved; you must make judgements about them. Many agencies use the services of part-time and freelance staff to supplement the full-time team. There is nothing wrong in this, provided the agency chooses such staff carefully and that the project is well managed.

The key in any project is the quality of the staff.

The agency may not only give you a list of past clients, but also suggest some that you could approach for references. Obviously, the agency will not suggest any companies who were unhappy with the work carried out, and for this and other reasons, references can only be a marginal consideration. Instead of taking up references, you can pick companies from the agency's general client list and ask for contact names. Remember, however, that the person who commissioned the research may have long since left. Also, any really dissatisfied clients are unlikely to be included in the list.

In summary, the information that should be obtained from proposing agencies is:

- How long the company has been established
- Whether independent or part of a group
- Turnover
- Number and skills of permanent staff and use of part-time or freelance staff
- Who will manage the project
- Areas of specialisation; either in terms of products/industries or research approach
- List of past clients

215

Proposals should at least cover all the elements of a research plan.

5. The proposals

The style and layout of proposals from different agencies will almost certainly differ, but they should at least cover all the elements of a research plan, as described in Chapter 1, in some form:

- Background to the research requirement
- Research objectives
- Information coverage
- Research methods
- Project management, staff and resources
- Reporting
- Timing
- Costs
- Experience

The *background* part of the proposal gives the agency the chance to show that it understands why you require the research and how the information will help you. The way this is approached may give you some clues on the agency staff's ability to get to the heart of a problem and understand your business needs.

If, in your brief, you have set a formal objective, the agency is likely to repeat this, perhaps verbatim. Similarly, if you have listed the required information coverage in some detail, the proposal writer may not be able to suggest any other areas to cover. However, signs of creative thinking might be welcomed here and, in any case, the proposal should at least confirm that all the areas you specified will be included.

The *research methods* section of any proposal is vital. You should be convinced that the approach proposed will provide reliable data in all areas. The methods planned should be described in some detail and include the following where relevant:

- The total number of interviews
- The structure of the sample and how it is to be selected – random, quota, judgement
- Who will be interviewed
- Type of interview – face to face, telephone, depth, group discussions
- Style of questionnaires – structured, semi-structured, checklists, the use of piloting

- If desk research is proposed, whether traditional library or computer data search and the expected time input for this activity

The agency's proposals may offer some alternatives in the methods section – in particular, a different sample size or method of interview. This is perfectly legitimate and gives you the opportunity to trade depth or quality of information against cost. The benefits of larger samples, or face-to-face rather than telephone interviews, should be spelt out. Similarly, a staged approach may be suggested in a larger project, with the option of terminating the project after initial research. This is particularly useful in new product or new opportunity research since a quite modest research input may indicate that the potential available does not justify further investigation. Obviously, a staged research approach does require, at least, verbal reports of findings after each stage, and time for you to consider the implications. For this reason, staged studies will take longer.

A significant element in the success of a larger project will be progress meetings with you, the client. This input should be defined in the proposal under research methods or elsewhere.

Two important additional comments should be made in relation to the research methods section of the proposal. Both concern what you *cannot* expect the agency to offer. The first is the submission of draft questionnaires with the proposal. Designing questionnaires takes time and is properly regarded as part of paid-for work. The second is that you should not expect to obtain individual respondents' questionnaires or, for that matter, any information about particular respondents. Agencies are commissioned to carry out a general study of a market or product and the responses from individual respondents are a means to this end. Just as you expect the agency and its staff not to reveal your company as the research sponsor (except with your permission), it is understood implicitly that information given to the research team by respondents is confidential to the research agency and goes no further in an attributable form. This important aspect of research companies' work can give rise to misunderstanding in some cases, because the proposal does not specifically spell out the principle. However, ethical agencies have a duty to respondents as well as clients and are bound by this rule.

Respect the confidentiality of the agency towards respondents.

The proposal should describe who will be working on the project – project management, staff and resources. You cannot reasonably expect that every individual working on the project will be named and profiled. Obviously, if a team of 50 interviewers are involved in a consumer survey, they will not be named. It may also be unreasonable to expect the agency to name all the key personnel, since if they are uncertain of the start date, they cannot be sure of individual staff's availability. However, the project manager should be identified and some details given of this person's background. Ideally, you should have already met this person. The skills and experience of other members of the research team should also be described, even if they are not named.

Where the work of 'executive' or 'consultant' level staff forms a major part of the project, you should expect the agency to indicate the man-day input of these members of the team. Almost certainly, the agency's costings will be partly calculated on this basis.

Ensure that it is clear what type of report is expected at the end of the project.

You should know from the proposal what *type* of report the agency expects to give you at the end of the project. Variations could include a full written report, a summary report with perhaps tables providing the detailed data, or tables or graphs only. Agencies will usually also expect to make some sort of personal presentation of the results, but it may be useful to have the degree of formality of this indicated.

The *timing* section should state how long, frcn the date of commission, it will take to complete the project. Possible dates may be given for both a verbal presentation of the findings and delivery of the full written report. If timetables are short, you may be able to act on the research after the verbal debriefing.

Costs should be definite and firm.

The *costs* of the research should be definite and firm. In consumer research, it is conventional to quote inclusive fees, covering all the agency's expenses, while in business-to-business research, it is fairly common to give a fee with a provision for variable costs (travel and telephone costs) on top. In the latter case (which often works in the interests of clients as well as agencies), some upper limit to the expenses should be indicated – for example, within a percentage of the fee. Terms of payment may also be stated in the costs section and it is normal practice for agencies to require a substantial deposit (up to 50 per cent of the whole fee) to be paid on commission. The justification for this is that the work can only be sold to the commissioning client and that, therefore, the security of a part payment is needed. While this is reasonable, it puts an additional onus on you to be comfortable with the soundness of the agency.

Clearly, the cost quoted by the agency is a very important, although not the only, consideration. If two proposals are similar in approach and you feel confident of the abilities of both to do the work, then it is sensible to select the cheaper. However, if one is considerably cheaper than another, you should consider why this is so. Possibly, the approaches may only *seem* to be the same and the agencies themselves have different views on what is involved. In these circumstances, you should seek further details from the companies concerned.

Often, proposals are not easily compared. The best approach may be initially to disregard the prices quoted and choose the best proposal (taking into account other considerations about the agencies). If you then find that this is also the most expensive, you may have to trade-off your expectations of quality against price.

You may find that all the agencies quote more than you had anticipated. If your budget is fixed, you will have to ask all of them, or perhaps just the one you favour, to suggest ways in which the costs can be brought down. Working together, in this way, the best compromise of quality and cost can be reached. Do not, as an alternative, simply ask the favoured agency to cut its fee without a corresponding reduction in input. Such bargaining may make you feel the tough buyer but the benefits may be illusory. An agency that has been squeezed in this way may be tempted to take short-cuts in the work.

The *research experience* section of a proposal gives the agency a chance to explain why it should be given the commission. Obviously, the best use will be made of any past work, however tenuous the connection with the project in hand, and some hyperbole must be expected.

Generally speaking, there is little point in asking market research agencies to make personal presentations of their proposals. If the proposal document is thorough, they can add almost nothing to what is set out in writing. True, such a presentation may indicate how good a performer the person from the agency is, but that person will not necessarily be the one who will make the final presentation. Further-more, it is the message rather than the style of the messenger that counts in the long run. A slick presentation of poor data only makes matters worse.

A more informal meeting with proposing agencies (or perhaps with the

219

one you most favour) to discuss their approaches may, however, be useful and is desirable for really large projects. You are bound to have questions of detail which are best covered at such a meeting.

6. The final choice

If you have followed our suggested approaches, you should now be able to make a confident decision based on:

- What you have learnt about the agency from meetings and visits
- The agency's proposals in relation to your initial criteria for agency selection

Obviously, you will let the successful agency know that you wish it to go ahead. It is also common courtesy to inform the unsuccessful agencies of your decision. They have, with good intentions, put considerable effort into their proposals and they deserve to know where they stand (if you have not already realised, the authors work in an agency).

Working with an agency

Arrange meetings with the agency throughout the course of the research.

Unlike general management consultants, market research agencies generally do their work away from your premises. If you wish, you may *not* have to see agency staff at all throughout the project. However, unless the timetable is very tight or the project very simple, you would be asking for trouble to take such a hands-off approach. A number of meetings may be required and a possible schedule is as follows:

- On commission
- To discuss detailed research methods, such as questionnaire drafts
- After pilot interviews (or particular parts of the interview programme)
- To discuss major findings before the full report is written.

Of these meetings, the first – the commissioning meeting – is the most vital. This gives an opportunity to review the research approach again and to discuss some of the details you could not reasonably cover before commission. At this meeting, you should also give the agency any information you have held back on grounds of confidentiality. This includes your knowledge or beliefs in the areas being investigated and, where relevant, data on your own company's sales. There is no point commissioning a study, at considerable cost, and then treating the agency as an adversary. They must be regarded as trusted, if temporary, colleagues.

As part of the commisssioning meeting, or on a separate occasion, you may need to arrange for the agency's key staff to receive a technical briefing, if product understanding is important (it usually is in business-to-business research).

Meetings to discuss detailed aspects of the research, such as sample sources and questionnaire drafts, can be very useful after the agency staff have done some initial work. In the case of questionnaire drafts, you should let the agency decide on the wording and structure, but you need to be confident that all the relevant areas are being covered. Also, you may be able to make a useful contribution in the more technical areas. A meeting after any pilot interviews will enable adjustments in approach to be made before it is too late. The agency staff will, however, need time not only to carry out pilot interviews but also to analyse the results from them.

An irritation to an agency is to be asked by the client, half-way through the fieldwork or just as it finishes, 'What do the results look like?' If a large programme of structured interviews is involved, agency staff will have no idea of the results until data processing is complete. Even in the case of a small-scale depth interview sample, covered by one or two researchers, the staff involved may have little idea of the overall picture; they will have concentrated on successfully achieving each interview. If pressed, they may give you a top-of-the-head impression, but this is dangerous. When the data is properly analysed, it may be that the findings are, in important respects, not as they have told you, but having committed themselves, they may find it difficult to give you a different and truer picture. For this reason, morning after debriefs from group discussions are undesirable. You may, of course, at the outset, agree to build into the research programme an interim analysis of results, but the agency will expect you to pay extra (because considerably more work is involved). Furthermore, there is still the danger that either the agency or you will be prematurely committed to data based on partial research. If you are going to ignore half the data, why pay for it?

Do not ask for results half-way through the research.

As part of working with the agency, you may decide to attend some interviews as an observer. This may be useful to give you some 'feel' for the research. Remember, however, that you will only see some of the

221

work and the picture will not be complete. Also, attending a few interviews is only a partial indicator of overall fieldwork quality; the agency will not send you out with their worst staff.

If they are systematic, agency staff will consider the research data in some detail before they prepare the written report or even plan presentation charts. At this pre-report writing stage, a meeting can serve a number of useful functions including:

- Alerting you to key findings that you or your colleagues need to act on immediately.
- Highlighting inconsistencies in the results, differences between the findings and other information you have or data that just seems doubtful. In these cases, the agency may need to back-check the data or even carry out further work. At this stage, it is important to work *with* agency staff to resolve problems rather than setting up a conflict situation. This even applies when you believe the agency has been negligent or incompetent. Recriminations can wait until later.
- To steer the final report. You should *not* expect to tell agency staff what to write but the emphasis in different areas can be tuned to meet your needs. After all, it is you and not the agency who will use the research. You can also reasonably impose some conditions on the length of the report and the use of tables and charts. If you know full well that your colleagues will never read a 100-page report, why have one written?

Evaluating an agency's work

When the project is finished, you should critically but dispassionately evaluate the work. This will affect whether or not you use the agency again and, in extreme (and we believe unusual) circumstances, may lead you to argue about the final bill. If you think there is a serious problem, you must have a meeting with the agency and discuss the issues. In any case, let them know your opinion of their work, including when you are satisfied.

The following checklist will help you to evaluate a project and provides a permanent record of your level of satisfaction:

- Extent to which the promised research methods have been carried out

- Level of coverage of the information specified in the proposal
- Confidence in the data provided
- Internal consistency of the data
- Agreement of the data from the research with other reliable sources
- Clarity of report contents
- How well the report conclusions are argued (and any recommendations if relevant)
- Overall quality of the written report
- Quality of the personal presentation

SOURCES OF HELP, ADVICE AND FURTHER INFORMATION

Government services

Business Statistics Office, Cardiff Road, Newport, Gwent NP9 1XG; 0633 56111

Central Statistical Office, Great George Street, London SW1P 3AQ; 071-270 6363

Companies House, 55–71 City Road, London EC1Y 1BB; 071-253 9393 Postal Search Section, Companies House, Crown Way, Cardiff CF4 3UZ; 0222 380107

HMSO Publication Centre, P O Box 276, London SW8 5DT; 071-622 3316 (orders), 071-211 5656 (enquiries)

Office of Population Censuses and Surveys, St Catherine's House, 10 Kingsway, London WC2B 6JP; 071-242 0262

Agents providing analyses of Customs & Excise data

Abacus Data Services (UK) Ltd, Causeway House, 24 South Drive, Coulsdon, Surrey CR3 2BG; 081-763 1000

Business & Trade Statistics Ltd, Lancaster House, More Lane, Esher, Surrey KT10 8AP; 0372 63121

Data Star, D/S Marketing Ltd, Plaza Suite, 114 Jermyn Street, London SW1Y 6HJ; 071-930 5503

Interactive Market Systems (UK) Ltd, Grosvenor Gardens House, Grosvenor Gardens, London SW1W 0BS; 071-630 5033

Maritime and Distribution Systems (Overseas Trade Data), 28 City Road, Chester CH1 3AE; 0244 46198

ABP Computer Services Ltd (for quarterly trade statistics at Standard International Trade Classification level only), Computer Centre, Hayes Road, Southall, Middlesex UB2 5NE; 081-573 5045

Database suppliers

Supplier of database	Name of database	Information within the database
Finsbury Data Services	Profile	Full text retrieval of media articles, e.g. *Financial Times*, *Daily Telegraph*, *Guardian*, and *Economist*. Also full text retrieval of Euromonitor, Mintel, McCarthy, Jordans and MSI.
Reuters	Textline	Full text retrieval of leading media sources in different geographical regions of the world, e.g. Africa, Latin America. Also full text retrieval of specialist industrial sources, e.g. banking and finance, property and construction, computing and electronics.
Dun & Bradstreet International Reporting Services	DunsPrint	Credit checking and financial accounts of companies all over the world.
Pergamon Financial Data Services	DunsMarketing	Direct mailing lists formed using complex search criteria.
ICC Online	ICC Viewdata	Financial accounts and information on UK and Irish companies. Also allows comparison of target company with the average performance of companies operating in that sector.
Reed Information Services	Kompass On-line	On-line version of Kompass directories. Covers the UK and most European countries. Also incorporates *Kelly's Directory*. Companies House data, Dial Industry, *Directory of Directors*. Allows the compiling of sample frames and mailing lists using complex search criteria.

Useful addresses

Advertising Association, Abford House, 15 Wilton Road, London SW1V 1NJ; 071-828 2771

AGB Surveys Ltd, The Research Centre, West Gate, London W5 1UA; 081-997 8484

BMRB, 53 The Mall, London W5 3TE; 081-567 3060

Dun & Bradstreet, 26–32 Clifton Street, London EC2P 2LY; 071-377 4377

Euromonitor Publications Ltd, 87 Turnmill Street, London EC1M 5QU; 071-251 8024

Market Research Society Ltd, 15 Northburgh Street, London EC1V 0AH; 071-490 4911

Marketsearch, Arlington Management Publications Ltd, 87 Jermyn Street, London SW1Y 6JD; 071-930 3638

Mintel International, 18–19 Long Lane, London EC1A 9HE; 071-606 4533

A C Neilsen & Co Ltd, Neilsen House, London Road, Headington, Oxford OX3 9RX; 0865 724724

Further reading

Kogan Page publish a wide range of books for business. A list is available on application to 120 Pentonville Road, London N1 9JN.